.

Last Stop: AUSTRALIA

A NEW VOICE OF THE HOLOCAUST

A memoir by

JOHANNA ALTMANN

Published in Australia by
New Homeland Publishers
ABN 27 405 493 873
Address: 39 Moorookyle Ave, Hughesdale, Vic. Australia
Tel: 0411566293
Email: eva@trainingpower.com.au

First published in Australia 2017

National Library of Australia Cataloguing–in–Publication entry
Altmann Johanna
Last Stop: Australia
A memoir by Johanna Altmann
A new voice of the Holocaust

ISBN: 978-0-9954325-0-5
ISBN paperback: 978-1-5446859-6-0 (Createspace version)
ISBN: 978-o-9954325-1-2 (eBook)

Cover photography by Bison United
Cover layout and design by B & J Designs
Printed by Ingram Spark
Typeset by Nelly Murariu, PixBee Design

Disclaimer
All care has been taken in the preparation of the information herein, but no responsibility can be accepted by the publisher or author for any damages resulting from the misinterpretation of this work. All contact details given in this book were current at the time of publication, but are subject to change.

The advice given in this book is based on the experience of the individuals. Professionals should be consulted for individual problems. The author and publisher shall not be responsible for any person with regard to any loss or damage caused directly or indirectly by the information in this book.

To my parents, who gave me the
values and determination to survive;

To my beloved children, grandchildren
and great-grandchildren;

I hope they can learn from my mistakes,
understand my past and appreciate
their wonderful life in Australia.

CONTENTS

INTRODUCTION

I was a born survivor and received a few important gifts into my cradle: good health, good luck and reliable instincts. Thanks to those precious gifts, I always managed to keep my both feet on the ground. I have won my battles even when I thought I was failing all the way. There always came a time when I could pick up the broken pieces.

PART 1
EARLY LIFE

My beautiful mother, Susi and I.

1

VIENNA IN THE 1920S
AND THE POLISH CONNECTION

To be born in spring in a city like Vienna is a special privilege. I arrived on 20 April 1923, the second daughter to my young parents Olga and Willy Altmann, a bit of a disappointment to my parents, who hoped for a boy. I was welcomed by my two-year-old sister Susi, who made it perfectly clear who was the "boss" and number one and kept in that way all the years to come.

I must admit, though, that she always cared and protected me and still is there when I need her.

My great-grandmother (Urgrossmutter Johanna), the revered and beloved head of the family, was on my side right from the start.

She took me in her arm, pressed me tenderly to her big bosom and decided that I should be named after her: "Johanna".

Nobody, least of all my mother, would have opposed her wish. They loved each other dearly. Thanks to her, my mother, a poor girl without a dowry, had been accepted into the rich Jewish family. My grandmother Sophie followed her mother's example and received her beloved oldest son's wife with open arms. I was so lucky to be born into such a loving family.

As "Johanna" seemed to be a bit too long and formal for a newborn baby, I was called "Hansi". Only my father called me "Hannerle". Both parents were young and beautiful. Mutti couldn't walk the street without being stared at and admired for her unusual beauty.

Neither of us girls could ever reach her looks. She was surrounded by love and luxury, having two nurses: one for Susi, Sister Wilma, and one for me, Sister Turner. For the housework, she had a maid.

Both grandmothers thought it was a hell of a job breast-feeding a baby, so they insisted that Mutti be served hand and foot. Papa, who was a young officer in the Austro-Hungarian army, continued his interrupted law studies after he got married.

He received a generous allowance to keep up this family standard. Great-Grandma Johanna had married into one of the richest families in Poland, Drohobycz.

The Lindenbaums owned most of the petroleum mines in Borysław and huge estates of land and forests. After her father died, Grandma inherited a large part of this fortune, as did her brother and sister. Her marriage to Grandpa Benedict Altmann was arranged, as it used to be in those old days.

Grandpa Benedict was a doctor of the highest military rank (General Stabsarzt, or "Surgeon General"); he came from the same Polish city of Drohobycz. A perfect match for the unattractive, fat but rich and good-hearted Sophie. So he brought his doctor title, his good qualities and knowledge into his marriage, and Grandma brought in her big fortune. They were wonderful, easy-going and warm people. Their marriage became a perfect one, and they loved each other sincerely.

Grandpa also was happy that his son had married the girl he loved. Like everyone else, Grandpa had been won over by her charm, beauty and intelligence. Although Mutti came from Kraków, Poland to marry her first and everlasting love in Vienna and missed her family in her home country, she adjusted quickly to her new life.

She learned the German language quickly but always kept her Polish accent, which made her even more charming and attractive. The famous Austrian composer Franz Lehar, who met her in Bad Ischl with Susi on holiday (before I was born), became a big admirer. At that time, he was working on his operetta *Das Land des Lächelns*. He kept assuring her how much he admired her beauty and pleaded with her never to lose her charming accent. Although their friendship was innocent (so she kept reassuring us), she inspired him in composing his operetta, which he completed in 1929.

My dear sister Susi took over as soon as I arrived home from the hospital. Not even the two nursing sisters were able to prevent her from showing her jealousy! She spat into my nappies with disgust and stuffed a spoon in my mouth to stop me from crying. Fortunately my nurse saved me from suffocation just in time. My Great-Grandma had a better way to stop me from screaming.

At the family celebration of my birth (there is no baptism in the Jewish religion, only the circumcision for boys), I had the special urge to scream. As it became more and more unbearable, Great-Grandma found a solution: she poured a few drops of wine on my lips and put me to sleep for hours, to my mother's alarm.

We lived in Döbling, an elegant suburb of Vienna with beautiful villas and parks. Born in spring on a sunny day, Sister Turner took me all done up in my beautiful pram for long walks. With her two protruding front teeth, she resembled a monster. Whenever she approached or even looked at me I screamed!

Otherwise she was so caring and perfectly trained that my parents had no reason to sack her just because of her looks. I probably got used to her later, but since that time, I have had a special fear of ugly people! I still don't like them today.

At a Friend's Wedding:
Susi the oldest and I the youngest Flower Girl.

2

THE GOVERNESS ERA

Ayoung, good-looking Kinderfräulein came
into our lives when nurses were no more
needed. I can't remember Sister Turner, of
course, but can still see Fräulein Elli very clearly
in my memory. I was quite aware of, but never
really accepted, the fact that my sister Susi
tried to get Elli's attention first and as usual
ruled over me. I forced myself into Elli's heart.
She sensed straight away who was everybody's
favourite, so she tried to give all her attention,
love and understanding to me.

It was obvious I was her Darling as Susi was Mutti's. Papa
never made any difference between us; we were both surrounded
with the same tender loving care.

Fräulein Elli was a trained kindergarten teacher and exactly
knew how to handle us both. She was the only one who understood why my sister made me so angry and always made me cry
and lose my temper.

She was aware of my jealousy as I had to play second fiddle to
my mother. She had a wonderful way to teach me how to control
my temper and was the only person I obeyed immediately.

I owe her my gratitude for my early upbringing. She read
beautiful stories to us, which I could listen to for hours. Elli

taught us how to care and share and how to speak properly. Not only how to use the language correctly but how to speak up and defend yourself. This taught me to enjoy reading and conversing without shyness. I am convinced that she developed our talents for foreign languages. Thanks to her I became an outspoken, confident, cheeky and funny little girl.

I probably can recollect those years with Fräulein Elli so well because they were the happiest years of my early childhood. I am convinced that my mother was a bit jealous of her. Not because of Papa, who never looked at another woman, but because she realised how much more I was attached to Elli than to her.

When I was four years old, my beloved Fräulein had to leave us, and my whole world seemed to fall apart.

Her successor was just the opposite of her.

She was a middle-aged (in my eyes then an "old woman") governess who only spoke French with us. We had to call her "Madame".

I hated Madame from the first day she set foot in our home. I wasn't over my heartbreak of the loss of my beloved Elli and was not ready to be taken over by this cold, bossy and ugly woman. I still can't understand today why my parents, particularly Papa, let her take charge of us. She was terribly demanding, sometimes even cruel and heartless. Of course, Susi again became Number One and took over the reins, together with Madame.

The first thing Madame taught us was how to fold the clothes at night that we needed to wear the next morning, neatly over a chair. Should we miss that sequence by even one item, if the jumper was put first instead of last, she dragged us out of bed, and we had to repeat the folding "her" way sometimes 10 to 20 times, depending on her mood. I got no help from my parents complaining about her; they were impressed by her educational expertise. Mum never interfered and Papa left it all to her. My good sister, of course, did everything right! I was the one who always got into trouble. I made life as unpleasant for her as she made it for me.

We were never allowed to talk at the dinner table. We had to "sip" water, not "drink". UN, deux, trois, she counted the sip and put the glass down. Our serviettes had to be folded after use in her special way; sometimes I had to do it three or four times until she was satisfied. Elbows under the table, cut the meat without a sound, put the chair under the table when leaving, these were her daily instructions: never to leave the table before her command!

We usually had our dinner in the nursery alone with her, and the maid had to serve the meal; she never lifted a finger. During her three-year stay, one maid left after the other. Nobody ever blamed Madame besides me. Who would have listened to a four- or five-year-old anyway? Her job was to teach us French and good manners, to take us to our music lessons and to supervise homework from school.

She looked after our wardrobe, so everything was extremely tidy and in order. Susi kept this tidiness, but I didn't. I always tried to annoy her by doing just the opposite. "Mouche toi au milieu", she commanded when we had to use handkerchief (blow your nose in the middle). I deliberately started always at the corner. Susi has kept the habit of blowing her nose that way until today.

When Madame had her "Ausgang" (day off), I felt like growing wings and flying out of my misery. I clung to my mother and behaved well without any problems. Papa took me for long walks or to the football, where he loved to go. Not that I have ever been interested in football, but being just near Papa was enough reward. I adored him, listened to his wonderful stories during our walks that were the highlight of my life then. I escaped when-ever I could from the tyranny of this witch. My sister didn't seem to suffer. She accepted all her orders, full of discipline, always eager to please and oblige.

In later years, she became equally obedient at school, agreeing with her bosses in Berlin and finally accepting the religious rules and traditions of her husband.

I became more and more rebellious and provocative, ignoring all the consequences. I tried to be as difficult as possible towards Madame. My greatest dream was to get her into trouble and to find a way to get rid of her.

My first revenge, of which I was very proud, took place in a hospital where my sister and I had to stay to have our tonsils removed. Not that I ever suffered from any tonsillitis, but Susi did.

Our specialist thought it would be a good idea to have us both done at the same time. The treatments for throat infections were so different then. Today it is a rare operation to have a tonsillectomy. The tonsils are there to protect against secondary infections and are kept until it's absolutely necessary to have them removed. Of course, nobody asked me for my opinion. I didn't even try to object as it meant a few days away from Madame, even if there was some pain involved.

The operation went well; under anaesthetic we didn't feel a thing. A lot of ice cream and plenty of presents from Grandma followed. Grandpa, as the family doctor, sat at our bedside, and we received every possible attention from our parents. It was heaven for me without Witch-Madame. I enjoyed it tremendously whilst getting stuck in my bowl of delicious mixed-flavour ice cream. But then Madame's face appeared suddenly over my bed, saying in French: "Eat slowly and don't mess up the bed!"

I put my bowl slowly on the side table: there was no rush, I enjoyed every move. I sat up straight in my bed, stuck my tongue out, as far as I could, with my still sore throat, stretched my fingers on my nose pointing out to her and let her guess what I thought of her. I knew she couldn't punish me in my hospital bed.

Susi of course was shocked, but everybody else was very amused. Most of all me! Even my mother laughed and forgot to tell me off.

Madame, who was unable to open her mouth from shock and embarrassment, walked out and never returned for the rest of our hospital stay.

I had planned a revenge for so long and finally I got it. God bless Doctor Suchanek, who had made it possible to have this operation. This event became a legend in the family circle. In particular Grandma told this story over and over again. I remember every detail and enjoy this memory tremendously.

Madame never forgot this embarrassing incident, which not only ridiculed her but undermined her authority. She made my life even more difficult than before. I kept on spying on her, convinced the day would come that I would be able to pay her back. As young as I was then, six or seven years old, I soon found out that she was very fond of booze. First there was her smell, which reminded me of my Uncle Jozsi, Papa's brother, who loved to empty Papa's schnapps and liquor bottles, which were kept in a cabinet for visitors. Papa hardly ever drank.

I caught her one day helping herself to a few hearty drinks from this cabinet. Once I had found her weakest spot, I never let her out of my sight.

One day she fell unexpectedly into my trap. Both, Susi and I went with her in summer for a short vacation, while my mother fell seriously ill with some kidney infection and Papa of course wouldn't leave her side. Papa took us to Hinterbrühl, a small country town where he rented a nice little cottage with a garden, only to leave us under Madame's "capable" supervision.

Now she felt free to celebrate with various bottles (there was a box full of them) in the evening after she sent us early to bed.

I never stopped watching her. I sneaked out of my own window and watched her sitting in her windowsill, every move. Susi never believed me when I told her about it. As much she wished she could "dob" me in, she somehow kept quiet.

Finally I convinced her to join me in the evening for my detective jobs, and she came out with me. As she was taller than

I was, her head appeared several times at Madame's window, watching her drinking accompanied by funny noises. One time, she couldn't stop herself from laughing out loud, and Madame noticed her. I quickly jumped back into my room through the window, into my bed pretending to be fast asleep. Well, poor Susi got punished by being locked in the dark garden shed and was told to stay there all night. My poor sister was scared out of her mind.

Madame kept drinking more and more until she fell asleep at the table, surrounded by empty bottles. As the owners of our cottage lived next door and Susi's sobbing became louder, I ran next door to call for help. The neighbours rang Papa immediately, and he arrived a couple of hours later by taxi. With the neighbours' help, we freed Susi, who was shaking and vomiting, suffering from shock. She and I were taken care of by these nice people next door until Papa arrived. He found Madame still completely drunk at the table, and to my never-ending joy and gloating, he sacked her on the spot.

Susi still felt guilty, whilst I felt like some hero on cloud nine. That was the end of the "Governess Era".

3

DER ANSCHLUSS:
12 MARCH 1938

It was one of those rare occasions when my
sister and I were peacefully sitting next to
each other, breaking cooking chocolate into
pieces, listening to the radio and munching the
chocolate. Our Federal Chancellor Kurt von
Schuschnigg announced his resignation to his
nation. I shall never forget that day.

Schuschnigg proposed a referendum regarding the annexation of our country to Germany. His speech was not only very
convincing but also emotional enough that we both cried.

Was that really happening, what they had been talking about
for weeks? Are we going to lose our independence, we wondered?
He pleaded with the media not to let it happen. He explained
to his Austrian citizens that he could not permit a civil war, no
blood to be spilled!

Hitler categorically prohibited the referendum. On 13 March,
President Wilhelm Miklas dismissed Schuschnigg from the
government and assigned Arthur Seyss-Inquart as his successor.

The very next day, German troops invaded Austria!

The following day, the "Anschluß of Austria" was officially
declared. President Miklas resigned, refusing to sign this declaration. The media was surprisingly ecstatic about these events.

They gathered in front of the Viennese Rathaus (Town Hall) and cheered "Heil Hitler" and sang the German National Anthem.

We were glued to the radio and spent sleepless nights listening. I was just turning fifteen; we were shocked and very scared. With our happy and secure life suddenly thrown into an unknown future, we stopped going to school. All of a sudden, the teachers, with only a few exceptions, plus most of our Christian friends, turned away from all the Jewish girls. We have never been confronted by anti-Semitism before in any of our schools. We had to attend an elementary school according to our home district and street. We could not choose which school we wanted to attend. I went for the first four years to a co-educational school, boys and girls from a poor background, lower to middle class with only a few from the "high society".

We were only three Jewish girls and two boys in a class of twenty-eight children. We blended in well together and had more Christian friends than Jewish ones. There was an Italian boy who talked in the most common Austrian dialect. His name was Rudi Duletti. He had terrible manners; I was scared of him when he used abusive language.

On my way to school, he used to hang out on top of the pole of a street light and call out to me: "Servus Altmann, you rotten Arsehole". As I never have been short of a reply, I answered him in equally rude language: "Hello you son of a bitch, just get lost!"

After a while we became good friends, swapping our lunches to our mutual delight. Rudi came from a poor family of eight children and always had the same lard sandwiches. I loved this simple bread, and he enjoyed my cold meat rolls or fine cheeses and fruit. After that pleasant bribery, we both walked nearly every day together to school, and he became my bodyguard.

From then on, I had never to fear the big boys again, and my walk from school was not only safe but also good fun.

I didn't like the school in Panzergasse, the dark corridors smelling from toilets mixed with disinfectants. With the school-mates I always got on well.

My sister, who was two years older and went to the same school, always frightened me before I commenced the new school year that I could be allocated to the class of the most feared and strictest teachers.

I even dreamt about it before I even started school. I was terrified. Would you believe that in fact I had to start this particular class? I couldn't hide my fear and "Mr Teacher" as we had to address him noticed this scary look in my eyes at once, him being an expert in "Beginners". To my surprise, Teacher Kropf turned out to be a wonderful, most understanding and fair teacher. I soon became his favourite pupil, the teacher's pet; soon he called me by my first name, which was not common in Austrian schools.

I returned his kindness by teaching him to swim when he took us to the compulsory swimming lessons. I had learned swimming when I was four years old.

Susi and I visiting our relatives in Kraków.

4

IN THE AGE OF ANTI-SEMITISM AND THE JEWISH DIASPORA

At the age of ten, I passed the entry exam to a private middle school, a well-respected girls' school, mostly supported by rich Jewish parents, although only a minority of girls were in fact Jewish. We had according to our religions different lessons in those subjects. Otherwise there was no hostility among teachers or class-mates or any anti-Semitic signs whatsoever.

This made the sudden change in their attitude in the days before the Anschluß even more surprising. It was the first time I had been confronted with anti-Semitism.

One of the schoolteachers came to our house to warn my parents about the new anti-Semitic wave, which worsened every day. Professor M. advised us to leave our school immediately in order to avoid harassment.

I was relieved, as I always disliked this school. My sister, on the other hand, took this change badly. She stayed at home and was depressed. I quickly adjusted to the new situation and kept in touch with my real friends.

My best friend Eva stayed as close to me as she had been for the last five years, although her parents had strictly forbidden her to mix with Jews. We always met secretly. Many of my Jewish friends left the country in a big hurry, leaving everything behind.

Even the shopkeepers at stores where we had shopped for years turned away from us. My mother was clever enough to dismiss the maid in time, not wanting to risk having an enemy amongst us.

One of my closest male friends, Bobbie, rang to say "Good-bye" as he was ready to leave for Teheran. His father, a rich businessman with worldwide connections, bought Persian citizenship for his family, Persia being a neutral country at the time. I never heard from Bobbie again.

Every day, another of my friends immigrated to a different part of the world. Not long ago, we had learned in the Jewish religious lessons about the "Diaspora" (dispersion in Greek) of the Jews dating back to the earliest centuries after Christ. Another Diaspora had commenced.

I had my eyes wide open, I listened, I learned and I observed. I soon realized that being Jewish was not easy to live with. It was the way I was born, nobody asked me or gave me a choice! There were so many questions in my head, but this was not the time to ask and receive answers. We had not been brought up as religious Jews.

My paternal grandfather, the Doctor who had served in the Army under Kaiser Franz Joseph as Surgeon General, felt more Austrian than Jewish. Grandma's family was divided into two parts: one very religious and the other non-religious and much more assimilated. She adjusted well to my grandfather's non-religious lifestyle, but they both kept some traditions. Grandpa was a wonderful man, loving and caring to all of us. He would sit all night at our bedside whenever any of us kids came down with a childhood disease like measles, chicken pox or whooping cough. He always knew a cure for everything. When the fever climbed as high as forty degrees and higher, he wrapped us in wet sheets, changing them right through the night. This cure I passed on in later years to my children and grandchildren. Whatever he did for us children was done with a minimum of fuss. I was only seven years old when he passed away and it took me a long time to come to terms with his death.

As young as I was, I have never forgotten him. After all these years, I still can see his face with his moustache and lots of broken veins in his cheeks. He had a General-like appearance with a heart of gold.

I have also wonderful memories of my Grandma; she was quite a lady! In my eyes, she was a queen. She had servants, a cook, a chambermaid and a laundrywoman. She did not even run her daily bath herself, I enjoyed the days I was invited to stay at her home tremendously. I got the same luxurious treatment Grandma received herself. The hairdresser called in every day to do her hair, and so she did mine as well. My mother was shocked every time I returned home to see all those curls done with an iron rod over a flame. My fingernails were painted just like Grandma's. At every visit, she took me to the best fashion stores for children to buy me clothes and toys. She was so gentle and never raised her voice. I respected, admired and loved her. She never used any other transport than taxi; she was such a fat lady that she probably would have been unable to fit into a tram. We were brought up to kiss her hand, one thing I have never been comfortable with. Grandma had a wonderful relationship with my mother, much better than with her own daughter. She took her along on her trips to the French Rivera in winter and to the most elegant holiday resorts all over Europe. Only the two of them travelled; we children stayed behind, cared for by Papa and the maid.

Grandma passed away one year before all the terrible events started to happen. She could never have coped with this new situation. Her late husband always warned her as a doctor that her abnormal obesity would be dangerous to her health. She wasn't a fighter either, so her illness progressed very quickly. My mother did not leave Grandma's bedside for months, and with the help of a private nurse, her last days in her home were taken care of with a lot of love and attention. It was heartbreaking for all of us to see her go at the age of 67, but as it turned out later, it was a real blessing for her. Grandma had always been a quiet, invisible support for us; she made sure we were brought up in a way that met her standards but was respectful of our wishes.

At the age of ten, I had one dream in my life and that was to become a dancer. My Grandma supported this dream ever since I was four. She paid for an expensive private ballet school with a leading dancer and choreographer, Grete Gross. Whenever we had a dance performance in one of Vienna's concert halls or theatres, Grandma was always sitting in the first row with a bright smile, clapping her little fat hands. She sent me always the largest box of my favourite chocolates to the stage by a messenger, treating me like a prima ballerina.

It took a lot of persuasion to convince my father to let me attend the Dance Academy. Papa never really interfered with our education; he left it entirely up to my mother to make the right choices for us. But becoming a dancer was in his view a *Disgrace*!

Finally, with Mutti's and Grandma's support, he agreed. I passed the test at ten instead of the usual twelve years old and had to work very hard to keep up with the older girls. It was my last year at the Academy when Hitler invaded Austria. The final exams were due in just a few months, and I would have graduated with a diploma. No more dreams to become a dancer, but I could live with that.

5

NEW HOME IN POLAND

Now there were far more important things to worry about.

A few days after the official annexation, the Gestapo arrested my father. Papa was a member of a Freemasons Lodge, which was not permitted under Hitler's regime. It was a non-political organization representing human rights. Papa was the treasurer of the Pestalozzy Lodge.

Two Gestapo men searched our entire apartment for money that they thought we had hidden at home. They did not know what they were looking for.

My mother immediately contacted our family lawyer, who was able to have Papa released after a couple of days. My parents were Polish citizens, and all my father's assets inherited from his mother were located in Poland. There was a law in Poland that no money could be transferred to a foreign country unless one was a Polish citizen. That's why my grandparents and parents never applied for the Austrian citizenship, although my father never learned the Polish language. Only on those grounds, the Gestapo released Papa.

My parents' decision to leave the country and immigrate to Poland came as a shock. Our maternal grandparents lived in Kraków, Poland, and we knew the country from our regular visits. My sister and I did not like it there. The only thing we agreed on was that everything was different there.

Most of all we hated the Polish language, and so did our father. No matter how hard my mother tried to teach us her native language, we refused to learn it. How wrong we were, we learned only later, far too late for Papa!

Kraków seemed a small village compared to Vienna. It was old-fashioned and conservative, a beautiful old city with a lot of history, but we were far too young to even imagine what life for us there could be like. My father was not happy about it either, but he had a lot of money invested in Poland, which he would never be able to bring to America, where most of his friends had chosen to immigrate.

My mother had her whole family in Kraków, which was another reason we went there. So "Good-bye Vienna", friends and relatives, we had to go. Before we left, our uncle Hans (husband of my father's sister) had been arrested. That was another big blow as we lived in the same house, and my cousin Hedi was my age. We also attended the same class at school and grew up together. We were on-and-off good friends, but there was a lot of jealousy between the families.

My uncle was not a popular man. He owned a well-established spice factory (still famous today for Hungarian paprika) and was a wealthy man. His factory workers hated him as he was rude and stingy, paid them poorly and sacked anybody if he disliked them. He treated his family the same way. He always had the idea that his children didn't deserve what he could afford to provide for them.

As far as he was concerned, there was nothing he would go without.

His house was full of rich visitors, and he kept the cook and maid busy day and night, parties going on all the time. He had one affair after another, particularly with underage girls. Aunt Lotte pretended not to know. He was too wealthy and powerful, and she had gotten used to this lifestyle, which she didn't want to give up. Their children suffered most under his domineering and abusive ways. My mother and father did not dare to interfere, but whenever there was an opportunity, they found an excuse to take my cousins under their wings, especially Mutti.

Hedi got punished on every minor occasion, which she never deserved. She had to stay in bed, even at the age of ten or older, and received only bread and water. I could not take all this injustice and always found a way to get food to her. My invention was "the Lift"; I hooked my schoolbag on a long rope and pushed it down through the window of the second floor beneath. Hedi then received the bag full of nice snacks and sweets, which made her life somewhat easier.

Mutti knew about it but pretended not to have noticed it. So did the neighbours, who lived on the floor between us, as far even putting up with the unpleasant noise when the bag rushed over their windows. We were not only thrilled to be able to help the poor children – there was also Hedi's brother Fritz, who was a bit slow and a bit weird, but a good-hearted boy in my sister's age – it was also a lot of fun. We also played cards this way when Hedi was grounded and had to stay in bed.

The sadistic uncle had somehow a weakness for me and liked me; whenever he saw me, he pinched my cheeks until I screamed. That was his way to show affection. He was the most feared and disliked man in all circles where he was known. With so many enemies, it was not a surprise that he was arrested in the early days of the wave of anti-Semitism. He was taken to Dachau and never returned.

Aunt Lotte was sent an urn with a note saying that her husband had died. My father was able with the help of another uncle from Poland, who was a clever lawyer and devoted brother-in-law, to send Aunt Lotte, Hedi and Fritz to England as quickly as possible.

We packed in a hurry to get away from all these dramas. To me it all seemed like a bad dream; we had no time to think, to cry or to realize that within a couple of months, we had been thrown in a completely different life.

Everything had to be kept secret; there was not even time to say "Good-bye" to our closest friends. Only our cousins and Aunt Lotte knew our plans. I loved her very much as she was very good to us.

So that was it; we left our wonderful childhood. We travelled by train to Poland. On the border in Zebrzydowice, my father was refused entry to Poland because although a Polish citizen, he had not been born there. He had been born in Austria, and that was the excuse given not to let more Jews into the country.

The anti-Semitic movement in Poland had grown over the last few years. Although not officially, they tried to make the life as difficult for Jews as possible. The authorities were unable to object to my mother's Polish documents and her ability to speak Polish fluently. My sister and I were underage and registered on her passport. We couldn't be separated from her, though born in Vienna as Papa had been.

How wrongly did we assume that we could escape Hitler by coming to Poland?

We were now confronted with a new problem. There was no going back! Papa insisted we should continue our trip, and he left the train after a heartbreaking "Good-bye". I sobbed all the way in the train until we arrived in Kraków. Papa was the person I loved most in my life. He was as fair and gentle as his late mother had been. I thought that my sorrow would never end.

My mother, an energetic and down-to-earth lady, convinced us finally that we had to trust and believe Papa would do the right thing and rejoin us soon. She was so strong and believed in God, as did my sister.

I had my doubts.

Grandpa picked us up from the train station in Kraków. Seeing his familiar face made me feel much better. He was a funny, small man with a moustache, which he cared for with much trouble and attention. This time the colour of his proudly kept moustache turned out to be green. My mother got a shock as his face seemed green as well. Thanks to him, our arrival was not as bad as we thought under the circumstances, but rather humorous. He took me in his short arms, cuddled and kissed me and joked about leaving my boyfriends behind.

Grandma received us friendlily but with more dignity. She never showed any emotion, even now. Her place, she thought, was in the kitchen, and the most important thing in life was *food*. She was a terrific cook. With the help of her maid, she never stopped fussing over meals, which appeared in an instant. That made me cranky right from the beginning, as eating was only a necessity but never a pleasure for me at all.

We lived cramped together; I immediately missed our large, comfortable home, and most of all, I missed Papa. Oh God, where was he?

I could not believe that my mother grew up in this old, ugly house in a predominantly Jewish area. In Austria, we hardly saw Orthodox Jews, but here I saw them everywhere. They wore long beards and side-locks, black caftans and "cappcles". They seemed to me like people from a different world. They were talking in loud voices, and it sounded if they were arguing all the time.

They bargained in Yiddish in the streets, the small shops overloaded with goods piling out onto the footpath. Grandpa showed us around. He was a well-known personality, a land-lord who rented out flats, taking his tenants to court when they fell behind in their rental payments. His son-in-law, who was a lawyer, had his hands full with all the court cases. Sitting in court was Grandpa's hobby and main occupation.

At the back of his house, there was a large storage room for his wholesale business in cane furniture. I loved this room with the particular smell of cane in which I could hide from all the noises of the busy street. I felt there, secluded in my favourite corner, feeling secure and having my privacy. There I could think and cry without being disturbed. I would sit in Grandpa's comfortable cane chair, reading and daydreaming, but most of all worrying about Papa.

It was also a hideaway from my sister, who ordered me around, and my Grandma, who always called me in for meals.

Only Grandpa knew about my secret corner and never gave me away. Sometimes he joined me with his daily drink of vodka, which he couldn't do without. He wasn't a heavy drinker, just liked a sip of "Youth", as he called it, to keep up with Grandmother's nagging. He supplied me with German books, which Grandma would never approve of, as it seemed not the right thing to read for a young lady from a good background.

Her father had been a Rabbi; she had his wisdom and a good but old-fashioned upbringing. Grandpa and I both did not approve of it. He loved to go to the post office, where he visited his favourite young girls behind the office counter. He called them all by the same name, regardless of what their real name was. He courted them in a humorous way; they all liked him, and nobody took him seriously. He was my best and only friend at the beginning of this new life. Without him, this new start would have been a disaster.

He soon realized that my sister tried to put me down and couldn't stand when I got any attention. She always had to be number one. She manipulated, stirred and organized me, and often I was blamed for things that weren't my fault. My mother always believed her and took her side, not like Papa. He was far too just for that. Grandpa, who was dominated himself by his wife, joined forces with me, and we became closer than I ever was with my mother. He was my confidant, and I listened to his advice.

After a couple of days, we received a phone call from Papa that he was safe and optimistic and would be joining us soon. What he told us seemed to me like a fairy tale, but I can assure you that it was a true story.

Susi and our mother taking a walk in Kraków,
wearing always hats and gloves. Polish women well known
for their excellent dressing style.

As I mentioned before, Papa was an active member of the Freemasons Lodge, which had branches all over Europe and America. They called themselves brothers without being Communists. To be fully accepted in this organization, they had to be trustworthy and prove their beliefs. They had to pass various tests at different levels to become a member. Full membership required using a secret sign language and taking a vow.

It took five years for my father to be appointed as treasurer of his lodge. This was a high and trustworthy position.

When he had left us at the Polish border, he had had no alternative other than catching a train back to Czechoslovakia as he was allowed transit for a few days. He booked a first-class train ticket to go to Prague, not really knowing where to go and what to do there.

He happened to share his compartment with a gentleman was friendly and elegantly dressed, and who spoke with a slight accent, similar to my mother's. Papa, who followed his instinct, started to use his lodge's secret sign language. To his amazement, the gentleman answered in a familiar way. Not only did he belong to the brotherhood, but also he was a Polish Consul in Czechoslovakia, the office being in Prague.

He invited Papa to stay at his house until he could clear Papa's papers for a safe return to Poland. This man was a well-trained diplomat and had to treat this matter in a careful and delicate way. My father would not even offer him a bribe. Instead he waited patiently in hope and confidence for a few weeks. He finally arrived in Kraków. What a reunion!

We knew – or *thought* we did – that nothing could stand in our way anymore to commence a new and well-protected life. Papa had full access to his mother's inheritance, which was quite substantial.

We immediately rented a furnished comfortable flat in one of the nicest outer suburbs. Eventually our furniture and all

other belongings arrived safely from Vienna. Our uncle organized everything, travelling back and forth to Vienna. He also
orchestrated the safe departure of Aunt Lotte and my cousins
to England, where a business associate of my father's helped
them to get settled in Cambridge.

However, my relationship with my sister, which never been
good, deteriorated more and more every day. My Aunt Genia,
Mutti's sister, generously offered for me to come and stay with
them. I gladly accepted and moved into Grodzka Street, which
was in the city centre. My cousin Alina, two years my junior,
was still a child. She went to a school wearing a uniform as all
the other Polish kids did, something we weren't used to in our
Viennese schools. She was a friendly young girl, so proud of her
Viennese cousins, and tried to imitate me in every way.

Now things had changed! I started dominating her and
teasing, which she certainly did not deserve, but after all the
years being put down by my sister, I thought it was my turn.

It was entirely my fault: we did not become friends then,
although Ala tried her hardest. Being an only child, she was
desperate for a sister. Both my uncle and my aunt never told me
how wrong I was!

They treated me with the same love as they treated their
daughter. They understood that I was going through a difficult
time adjusting to our new way of life. They made my stay in their
home so pleasant that in the end I did not want to leave when
we finally got our own luxurious apartment.

Our new home was much bigger, more elegant and more
luxurious than the one in Vienna had been. Mother, with her
exceptional taste, decorated our new home, which consisted of
six large rooms and a modern kitchen with more space than half
of our Viennese flat. The bathroom was a dream, a long hallway
with lots of built-in wardrobes – something you did not see in
many apartments those days. I got my own bedroom at last.

All arrangements were made for her to go to study in England. Susi was looking forwards to her departure as much as I was to getting rid of her. The thought of it made us more tolerant towards each other.

We walked together to explore Kraków, suddenly discovering this beautiful city. Kraków was surrounded by a circle of gardens called *Planty*, so big that one could walk there for hours. We were surrounded by the smell of flowers and fresh grass, a spectacular sight, which attracted both tourists and the city's own population.

We also ventured near the grounds of the Old University, trying to meet some of the attractive students. We both were used to going out with boys and missed their company. That area and the gardens were the best places to make some acquaintances.

We attended together private Polish language lessons taught by a conservative Jewish teacher. The first sentence we learned in Polish was "I don't talk to strangers".

I don't remember having to use this phrase ever! Nevertheless we waited until the boys approached us first. We soon were well known as the two sisters from Vienna, always dressed very chic, thanks to our mother who was talented and full of good fashion ideas. We both enjoyed this attention, heads turning around and young men courting us. As we were lonely and had no friends, we stuck to each other and became a bit closer. Our voices were almost identical, and even now in our late seventies, we both sound the same.

We used to play tricks on the phone when our admirers rang. Susi would start the conversation and I finished it, or the other way around. When one made a date, the other turned up. We had lots of fun and soon became accustomed to our new life. I forgot about Vienna and did not feel homesick or miss anybody. I refused to go back to school, always having the excuse of not knowing Polish well enough. Susi studied English extensively as she prepared herself for her new school in England.

As much as I disliked the Polish lessons and my teacher, I did love my private English lessons with good old Miss Allen. Her English was perfect, the same pronunciation we learned at our school in Vienna. She was a funny old spinster, always dressed in long floating robes, her hair dyed in all different shades from blond to red.

She could also palm read, and she read mine without charge. She liked me so much that she tried to warn me about my future. First she told me, with slight disgust, that I was going to have far too many men in my life, even more than one husband. How right she was! Then she told me that I was going to travel a lot, and my life would be full of storms. These were her exact words. I have remembered them all my life. Everything she told me turned out to be true, although I have never believed in fortune telling.

She was a terrific teacher; my school English did not include proper conversation. She taught me the basics plus a lot of grammar, which came in handy for conversation with Miss Alpen's proper English. I also learned about English culture, literature and customs, which fascinated me. Her lessons were never boring, and neither was my life.

"*Nie ma nic zlego, co na dobre nie wyjdzie*", Mutti always used to say: "There was nothing so bad that would not turn out to be even better". So my new start turned out to be far more interesting, exciting and surprising than I had expected. Vienna was definitely behind me.

This chapter was now closed, no regrets!

For the time being, Mutti tolerated my wishes not to attend school. She was always ready for a compromise and never forced us into doing something we did not like. But she made it clear that I had to do *something*.

Of course, my first thought was to continue with ballet, but my father objected strongly and this time he put his foot down. Mutti sided with Papa and her mother, all against me. How could two grandmothers be so different? In order to please Papa, I did not persist with this and accepted their decision.

Finally I went to a private fashion design school to learn dressmaking, It was not my cup of tea at all.

Firstly I did not have any talent for it, either drawing or sewing. I kept attending the school to kill time and keep my parents happy. I met nice older girls and young women there, who helped whenever I had difficulties. The teacher and owner of this school was young, good-looking and understanding. She was one of my uncle's relatives, but never told anyone how unsuitable I was for that trade. You can imagine my surprise twenty-three years later I ran into her in Georges' department store in Melbourne, Australia, where I worked at the perfumery counter of Christian Dior and recognized her immediately. She still was such a good-looking woman.

I enjoyed the company of girls at that school and all their attention just because I was a Viennese girl. We went to the swimming pool, where we had the best opportunity to meet some interesting boys. With my training in swimming and Susi's diving, we found it easy to turn the heads of some good-looking men.

Very few Polish girls or women could swim in those days, so we had something to show off and did we ever! Whenever a good-looking male appeared that we fancied, we dived into the pool. Unfortunately Susi and I had the same tastes in men. We both liked ones much older than we were, and the younger boys we ignored.

Again from now on, we went our separate ways. I made friends with the girls from the dressmaking school who intro-duced me to their brothers. I was often invited to their homes and spent my time with them. I learned about social life, how to behave with men and playing "hard to get". I practiced all the games I learned from those older and more experienced women, and to my delight, it worked.

Mutti always allowed us a lot of freedom as long as we stuck to the rules. She had to meet our friends and approve of them, which never was very difficult. Another rule was "Not to kiss in the lift", as Papa once saw me and got very upset.

"Bring your boyfriends home", she said. You have your own room and don't forget to close the door, so Papa won't catch you. We had a most understanding mother; we were so lucky!

Papa was like most fathers are with their daughters: protective but far more conservative. He left it to Mutti to keep us in line. Mutti was a happy person, full of energy to make our life so pleasant. Fully contented now, finally living in her own country with her family, parents and friends. We never realized before or ever asked if she been homesick marrying Papa when she moved to Vienna.

Our recent experiences and disappointments in Vienna with anti-Semitism taught us to mix only with Jewish friends. There we did not need our parents' advice. We now felt at home and never enjoyed life more than in those days of summer 1938.

Kuba, the Love of my Life.

6

LOVE IS IN THE AIR

I was invited to my cousins' school camp at a well-known holiday resort. As the girls were all much younger than I, the teacher appointed me to become the assistant to the sports instructor. We shared the same room and became good friends immediately. Hela was a lovely twenty-year-old woman, who also shared my interest in the opposite sex. I helped her supervise the youngest group and instructed them in swimming. I remembered well the days in elementary school when I had taught my schoolteacher the backstroke. The girls all liked me, and we had lots of fun together.

Nevertheless, I was greatly surprised when a good-looking, much older man seemed to be watching me and eventually tried to chat me up. At first, following the instructions of my girl-friends from sewing school, I played "cool" and not interested in him at all. It was not easy to play this game as I was dying to go out with him, but to my greater surprise, he was determined not to give up. He must have found out from the young girls where we were staying and turned up one evening at the camp to ask me out.

Hela helped me to dress in her nice, modern clothes, making me look very grown up. His name was Kuba; he was ten years older than I and was spending only the weekend at this resort while travelling between Kraków, Katowice and Łódź.

We spent two days together, and I fell in love with him immediately. He promised to come back and see me again! Just in case I gave him my address and phone number in Kraków.

The next day Papa arrived by car for a visit. Papa, being my most loved and important person, was a wonderful distraction from the now-boring camp. He was eager to take me back home with him. I thought it would be a good test for my new acquaintance to see if Kuba was as interested in me as I was in him. I did not really believe that he would come back to see me, a view shared by Hela, my friend and confidant.

A few days later, I received a letter from Kuba expressing his great disappointment that I had not waited for him. He worked for a big company in Łódź and came every weekend to Kraków. A great romance started. He was such a handsome, charming man; who could ever resist him?

Mutti invited him to dinner, and her impression of him was not the same as mine. She thought he was too old and, as a travelling salesman, not a good match for me. She did not approve of him. Papa, on the other hand, liked him as he was witty and intelligent, and trusted him more than my mother did.

After a while, she got used to him and probably was taken in by his charm as everybody else was. When he told her in front of my sister and me that no one could compete with her beauty, she finally gave in.

I think that he meant what he said, as my mother was such a beautiful woman, famous in Kraków. This made me proud of her, as opposed to my sister, who was jealous and tried to compare herself to her. Susi was an attractive girl, but far from beautiful. Neither was I, which did not bother me.

From the beginning, Susi's relationship with Kuba was hostile. She resented it even more that he did not take the slightest interest in her. When Kuba and I started to "go steady",

I lost all interest in other men. My good friend, Andzia, had a holiday house in Rabka, not far from Kraków, and she invited us as often as possible to stay there on weekends. I knew her from my days at the fashion school; she was much older than I and a clever young lady. She allowed us a lot of privacy as she trusted Kuba would not take advantage of the situation. He never tried! We kissed and cuddled, but that was it. On my sixteenth birthday, I received a long box sent by courier, and my mother was convinced it was a doll. As this package came from Łódź, I knew it must have been from Kuba. He always called me "Baby".

At first I was furious at the thought that he would send me a doll, but to my surprise, I found sixteen gorgeous red roses with a card telling me how much he loved me and how serious his feelings for me were.

I believed him, Mutti was confused, Papa bemused and my sister green with envy. This was my first great triumph over her. We had a big party in our apartment, thrown by Mutti, prepared by the cook and maid. Invited were my sister's friends, among them Julek Holzer, Susi's boyfriend. He was an ugly but rich businessman, well known in the Jewish circles. Julek congratulated me sincerely on the choice of Kuba, and they became friends almost immediately. Susi was so annoyed about it that spoiled the whole party for me. My understanding parents left that evening to stay with Mutti's sister until late. At two a.m., they telephoned to ask if it was O.K. to come home? Unfortunately this dream life did not continue for long. Mutti always said it was too good to be true.

Kuba took a few days off to stay with me. We went swimming and dancing, and had a wonderful time together. One day, he took me to meet his friend Stasiek, who had just gotten married. Kuba bought large bags full of delicacies, fruit and cakes and explained to me that the young couple did not have much money. Stasiek, in his last year of medical school, earned his living by tutoring high school students, and his wife got a small allowance from her parents. We turned our visit into a feast for them, as they kept assuring us without being embarrassed. They were still on their honeymoon and talked freely about their sex life.

In my day, everything connected with sex was a big secret. Of course I knew about it; Mutti told us whatever she thought we were supposed to know at ten years old. I always had my eyes wide open and listened to all sorts of conversations that I was not allowed to hear. As I mixed with older girls, some of whom were already married, I heard a lot but was still pretty innocent. I read books and magazines full of love stories. Our maids in Vienna always filled me in on what I wanted to know. Still I could not completely understand what this young couple was talking about. On the way home, I asked Kuba for explanations. I wanted to know what part in a marriage sex life really played.

Kuba became very serious, something I was not used to from him. He always joked and laughed, treating me as the teenager I was. "You really want to know?" he asked. But yes, of course, where else could I get all the answers from?

"Marry me", he said totally out of the blue, "and you will find out", taking me in his arms. I thought he was teasing me again, but in fact he was dead serious. How could I, even if I wanted to? I was far too young. Papa would never agree. "Well, he said, "I just wait for you, whenever you are ready". I was not sure if he really meant it when he said it or if it was just a romantic mood after seeing this young and happy couple. I did not say a word the whole way when we walked home together. When he kissed me "Good-bye", I looked at him and asked if this meant we were engaged? I just could not believe that I, the younger daughter, living in my sister's shadow, just received a marriage proposal! I was only sixteen; it just couldn't be true. As it turned out later, he meant every single word.

We both agreed: it would be best not to tell anybody about it yet. That was the hardest part for me as I felt this incredible urge to tell everybody including Papa, Mutti and most of all Susi. I did not even dare to divulge my secret to my best friend Andzia as I was afraid she would not take me seriously. So we kept this big secret, and I kept living on cloud nine! Repeating constantly Mutti's words: it was too good to be true.

The perfect life we had lived for the past one-and-a-half years could not last forever. It just was not meant to be.

PART 2
World War II Years

7

ON THE WAY TO DROHOBYCZ

Hitler started to stir again, this time right here in Poland. He demanded access to the Polish corridor. Danzig should be free again, rather than included in the German Reich. Poland was not as quick to surrender to him as Austria and Czechoslovakia; Hitler had a good excuse to start the war, and Marshall Rydz-Smigly, who led the Polish army, mobilised the country.

So where did that leave us? My parents decided with my mother's family to move away. They did not believe a Polish victory was likely, as the army was ill-equipped for a war. "It is going to be a Blitzkrieg", my father said, "we will return soon"! My grandparents refused to join us, and nobody objected. How could they have been left behind? I could never understand that.

My father's much younger brother Jozsi had lived with us ever since he left Austria sometime after we had. He was a *no-hoper*, heavy smoker, alcoholic and morphine addict. He never worked in his life. My exceptional Viennese grandparents had taken him the way he was and did everything they could help him change in their loving way, without much success.

After their deaths, Papa took over taking care of him in the same loving way. Unfortunately due to his extreme smoking and drinking habits, he suffered from severe vascular disease. He had "smoker's leg", dangerous blood poisoning, which led eventually to amputation of that leg. My parents went through absolute hell with him. Otherwise he was a handsome and good-natured person, paradox as it may be, loved by everybody. Women were crazy about him. He had affairs, one after the other for many years when his parents were still alive. He inherited the same amount of money and assets from his late parents as my father did. He was a rich bachelor without any commitments or obligations, so he spent his money in his abnormal way. Nobody could stop him. He had a private nurse, who wheeled him around in the wheelchair, was friendly and generous with everybody and hardly had any enemies. My parents thought he would be safe in our comfortable home with our devoted maid and a male nurse and of course with plenty of money. Our departure was only temporary; that's what everyone thought.

I had only Kuba on my mind. He would have to join the army, and there was no way in getting in touch with him. I left messages everywhere and hoped he would call to find us. We planned to go to a small town in Galicia to stay with some other relatives. I left the address behind for him. As the army confiscated all private cars, we left by train only a few days before World War II started on 1 September 1939.

We took the train to Przemysl carrying only a few suitcases with us. It was one of those glorious autumn days typical in Poland. It made the whole escape a bit easier. Nevertheless I cried all the way during our trip, this time over Kuba.

I was more furious and rebellious than sad. Why did we have to run again? What was so wrong with being Jewish?

My family and all my Jewish friends were good and honest people. What made us so different from the other races? Life had just started to be so beautiful surrounded by so much love, security and excitement. I was at the peak of my young life, and here I was once again, on the road to an uncertain future. When we left Vienna eighteen months ago, at least we had known where we were going. I trusted my father and his clever instinct, I believed so much in him, but this time I was very confused. I had my doubts if this time he had made the right decision. I had no choice, which also contributed to my frustration.

Our arrival in Przemysl was accompanied by chaos. The town was under constant attacks of gunfire and bombs. We found our destination empty. Our relatives already had flown before we arrived. They at least left a message and the keys to their apartment with a friendly Polish neighbour. Most of the time, we had to stay in a cellar to hide from the fury of the bombing raids. I carried Kuba's photo with me day and night, hoping I would soon hear from him. Suddenly, the attacks started to subside. Papa called it "peace before the storm", but it gave us a break.

My sister and I tried to get hold of some Polish soldiers to organize food. We were lucky enough to buy some bread, sugar and sausages from them. Some older officers provided us with more luxurious stuff like sardines, jam and chocolate. It was enough to survive. Some of the food stores were still open, and for a huge amount of money, after queuing up for hours, we brought home whatever we were able to get. Later on, we were able to exchange our luxury goods for bread.

The weather was still beautiful, warm and sunny, and we were wearing our pretty summer dresses. Susi and I came home in good spirits after our successful shopping spree. Papa stood at the door with a bright smile that I hadn't seen on his face for a long time. I thought he was going to tell us some terrific news like the war being over and we could return home. But there was a surprise.

He ordered me into the kitchen to put away the shopping. "Mutti wants to see you right away", he said, "hurry up!" He made sure Susi remained with him. Why all the secrecy? What had I done? Looking at my father's face, there was something to look forwards to. I did not expect in my deepest imagination, even in my dreams, what I saw now.

Standing in front of me was a tall, handsome soldier, revealing his beautiful white teeth smiling at me. He held his arms wide open, and we held each other hugging, laughing and crying. I could not believe my eyes. It was Kuba.

He could get away from the army only for a few hours and had to report back to his battalion. We were standing on the big terrace in the bright sun, holding hands, talking and making plans. He assured me that he would not remain a minute longer with the army, which he had been forced into joining. He thought it would be only a matter of weeks until the Polish army would be beaten.

Papa gave Kuba a few addresses with contacts in Lemberg and Drohobycz, just in case he needed them.

We were waiting for a transport to continue our trip to Drohobycz, the town in which Papa's family's assets were located, and were ready for financial settlement. That was our original plan. Hitler united with Russia would never be able to claim that side of Poland for the time being, at least.

Letting my man go broke my heart again. My only comfort was that I could trust him to come back. I was sure of his love and intentions.

My mother was not too pleased by his arrival. She thought it was one of those short episodes, which Susi and I had at numerous times, as happen to young girls. Falling in love once again, nothing too serious, she hoped. A man ten years old than her sixteen-year-old daughter would never take her seriously. Seeing him here again, she realized how wrong she had been. On the other hand, Papa, who was always far more old-fashioned and reluctant concerning our boyfriends, was this time much more understanding than usual. He truly liked Kuba.

Kuba was able to supply us with more food, enough to last us for weeks. There was no transport available besides a horse cart with two old tired horses. The owner of this transport was a shifty peasant, who demanded a fee that he probably could not have earned with hard and honest work in a year. My father and uncle, who organized this coach, did not trust this man, but we had no choice. The town we were leaving was a battleground. The next day, Przemysl was destroyed.

I will never forget the trip to Drohobycz. Sitting on the top of our luggage, we could not move without fear of falling. We were sitting on an open platform, which normally transported cattle or hay with no seats or roof. We were lucky, as the days were still warm and sunny, but the nights were freezing; we were a family of seven, my aunt and uncle and Ala their daughter and all of us.

We all huddled together to stay warm in the night, covered with filthy-smelling horse blankets. Actually we were lucky to be on this cart, as we watched the roads full of people walking, dragging their belongings every day. The people, mainly Jews of all ages, young children, tired old men and women, almost with their last strength pushing forward. We took turns and let some of those poor refugees get into our cart and swap our seats, walking to warm up. We took some of their luggage, which they were unable to carry, exhausted, hurried and desperate. My father and uncle carried some of the small children, sometimes for hours. We met Polish officers on the road, who were deserting the army and running away. They still had cars and jeeps, so they sometimes picked up women and children and some very old people, who just could not make it any further. The bombardment from the sky followed us. During the day, the aeroplanes flew so low we could see the machine guns. They fired into the crowds. Sometimes people could not find cover quickly enough, and they were killed on the road and their bodies left behind.

My father, having served in the First World War as a young lieutenant, took command of our group. He ordered us to jump out of the cart into trenches and lie flat covered with branches. No time to think or be scared. We had to move on. In the middle of nowhere, the shifty cart owner stopped and refused to take us further unless we paid him twice as much as he had already received. My father and uncle tried to reason with him to no avail until a big argument started. Military vehicles were passing, some of them nearly empty. My sister and I were standing on the road, waving to stop them, hoping some of them would be able to take us. Finally a big truck with a few soldiers slowed down and offered some help. When they heard about the way the man had tried to blackmail us, they all jumped out and packed our luggage and all of us into their truck; before we knew what was going on, we had already moved on, leaving the startled horseman behind us. The soldiers with an older officer were on the run themselves. There was no hope for the Polish army to win. We headed on to Lemberg (also called Lwów), where my parents had a few addresses to stay for a start.

We were terrified as we entered the city. We saw houses completely destroyed, without roofs, windows, and walls in pieces.

One could see bathtubs and stoves hanging out of the windows and loose wires everywhere. Between broken glass, shells and ruins all over, there was the sickening smell of dead horses, cats and dogs.

8

THE SMELL IN A CELLAR

The sky over the city glowed red from fires. The smell of smoke and decay crept into the nostrils up into the eyes. So that was war. You can't imagine when you read about it or have seen it in a movie. The streets were totally deserted; the whole civil population lived in cellars.

There was no water and no electricity. The local people had stocked up on groceries and food, and we were lucky to have still some sugar cubes, bread and the tins, chocolate and sweets Kuba had brought. All I could think and dream of was a clean bed to sleep in.

Papa and Uncle organized a place in a cellar to stay until they found the friends they had been counting on. We got one dirty old bed for the seven of us and took turns sleeping in it. Not me! I would have rather occupied one of the chairs before I could lie down into the smelly, disgusting mattress.

So there we were.

No home, in the middle of a battlefield, completely disoriented. But, as they say, where is life there is hope. At least we were still all together. But for how long?

My parents found a place to stay with a German couple. The man stayed with us in Kraków for a few months, until he joined his wife in Lemberg. He was Jewish, and we had taken him in as a refugee from Berlin into our home. So they now returned the favour. The whole family decided, as the Germans were so close, to send our father and uncle away, near the Rumanian border. Women were safer, everybody thought. Once again an emotional "Good-bye"; for me again, the worst thing was to see Papa go.

The four of us stayed in a small room with one huge bed where we all fit in, pressed to each other like sardines. The bombardment of the German Luftwaffe – air force, artillery fire – continued. Tiger tanks approached the suburbs. The whole city shook with the roar of the guns. The Polish Army still was trying to defend the city with the help of the population. Susi and I mixed with the crowd to build barricades and trenches.

The city's civilians spent most of their time in cellars. At the short breaks of explosions and detonations, we queued up for water and Susi was always close to me – the right team at the right time chatted up soldiers in order to organize some food. We were always lucky; it was amazing what luxury items we brought "home". We built up quite a storage, which we used again as an exchange for the missing groceries. Our bargaining business flourished; it was as exciting as it was dangerous to be strolling the streets under constant fear of being killed.

When you are young, you are more optimistic and think positively. I don't recall being scared of anything in those days. My worries were for my father and Kuba. Not knowing where they were and if they could survive put me into a greater panic than the fear of losing my own life. We just lived day by day.

After two weeks, rumours were spreading that Lemberg was supposed to be levelled to the ground. No hope to get out alive from this battle! Hundreds of exhausted Polish fighters surrendered the city. It was mid-September, and the Jewish New Year started, followed by Yom Kippur, the Day of Atonement. Suddenly, there was an unusual silence. No bombardment or heavy artillery. No sound outside the cellars. "This is the beginning of the end", I thought. Peace before the storm.

I had been sitting in a dark corner of the cellar with Kuba's photo pressed to my heart; this photo was worn out from all the kisses, tears and sticky hands. He stood upright, showing his beautiful white teeth with a big smile. Was I ever going to see him again? What was happening to our lives? I hadn't been scared and afraid to die. I had been so angry, confused and full of doubts. Had my parents made the right decision to run away the second time to leave our home, our belongings and everything? As young as I was, I had realized that there was no such thing as security.

Jewish people in the cellar lit some candles; after all, it was our holiday. They prayed, some of them silently devoted, others crying loudly, hysterically almost, in panic.

The smell in this small cellar was awful. A mixture of mildew, perspiration and musty, fishy smells from dirty bodies. Who knows, I thought, how long we are going to stay here? It looked like we wouldn't be able to get out from this place for a long time, according to all the outside messengers. Prepare yourself for the "worst", they told us.

This unusual silence explained as a pause before the worst attack was more nerve-wracking than the loudest bombing. I missed Papa; he would have given me some explanation or comfort. Still holding Kuba's photo, I cried myself to sleep. I must have slept for hours.

9

THE RUSSIANS ARRIVE ON YOM KIPPUR

When I woke up, I couldn't hear a sound or see anyone in the cellar. They were all gone. "Oh my God", I sobbed. They had all died, and I was the only one left. I pinched myself to make sure I wasn't dreaming or was dead? I pulled myself out of my corner; it was dark, and I hardly could see or hear a thing. There was an emergency light over the exit of the cellar, which had helped me to find my way out. Bright daylight greeted me, and my eyes hurt after the long days of darkness. I heard some voices, which became louder with every step I took. I did not dare to call out; I had no idea what was going on.

As I walked up the stairs, I imagined I had heard my mother's voice. They were all dead! No, I hadn't lost my mind, it was really her. She was just on her way to get me, she said. "We thought we had better let you sleep, you were so exhausted". Mutti took me in her arms, hugged and kissed me and told me a story that I could not believe. The Russians came to our rescue. They took over the city and the part of Poland from the other side of the river.

They have been a Godsend, Mutti said, on our Jewish holiday Yom Kippur. I think I still believed then in miracles.

A rich Jewish family invited us all to their traditional holiday dinner, which was a real feast. There was so much to celebrate. The war was over; we were alive and full of hope of being reunited with Papa and Uncle. I was relieved, of course, but far from happy. What about Kuba? Did he survive the war? What now? We were still homeless; the city was one big disaster, with a shortage of housing, food and water. There were hardly any men around to do the heavy jobs of cleaning up the streets from their ruins. No transport, no communication. No more cellars – that was something to be grateful for. At last we could change our clothes and clean ourselves. We were full of head lice we had caught in the cellar. My mother started a radical cure with petroleum, which was used for cellar lights. It served another purpose too; the smell of it was so strong that it would have kept the Russian soldiers away from us.

There were rumours and fears of rape, abuse and burglaries committed the Russians. We locked ourselves in for days until the situation calmed down; it didn't take long until food and water supplies had been organized. Times must get really bad to appreciate little things like that.

I can't say we got on with our lives; we rather stayed alive to battle on. My mother, who did not lose her energy, carried on and coped well with everything. She organized a better place to stay for us, although it was extremely difficult, as people had to live in ruins. The constant arguments between us teenagers and my mother and her sister did not improve this whole situation, but Mutti never let it get out of control. She managed perfectly without showing how much she missed Papa. So did I!

We queued up half a day for the most basic items available. To my surprise and joy, I met in those endless queues a few good friends from Kraków. Some were Kuba's friends, too.

It was not after all such a crazy idea of my parents to pack and run. We were not the only ones. I was able to collect not only news about people I cared a lot about, but also plenty of hints and good advice in order to exist. We existed in those days;

you hardly could call it "living", Still, I never stopped worrying about Papa and Kuba and missed terribly grandpa in Kraków.

When Papa returned with Uncle Gutek, life looked a bit more promising. The four of us moved on to the town of Drohobycz, where his parents' estate was located. Aunt Genia, though, decided to stay in Lemberg with her husband and daughter. The big mansion belonging to my grandmother's family for many generations had been taken over by the Russians and was being used as their headquarters.

I took an immediate dislike to this small town. Everybody knew everybody, in particular, Grandma's family name "Lindenbaum". They had been successful, rich and well respected. They owned not only the major oil sources but also land, forests, real estate all over the town and their neighbourhood like Borysław, Truskawiec, Tarnów and others. They were highly educated doctors, lawyers and businessmen. It was a generous family.

In 1939, when the war was to start, they donated an airplane to the Polish army. Herr Spanndorf, the Administrator of the Estate employed by my previous three generations, was a kind and wise old gentleman. His devotion to the family had been genuine and honest, though a bit embarrassing for my modest upbringing. We were never told back home in Vienna about the financial status of our family and had no idea how wealthy they were.

It was the first time we heard about it in detail from Herr Spanndorf, who was a real storyteller. His pockets were filled with sweets for the children, wherever they came from, and cigarettes for friends.

Herr Spanndorf spoke German with a specific Jewish accent mixed with Jewish words, which I found amusing. I liked this old gentleman, the only one, as the others were absolute strangers to me. My grandfather's sisters were not a bit like him. I think the admiration I had for the old Herr Spanndorf had been mutual. He made sure I could live in the nice, elegant house of his daughter and her husband, a solicitor, Dr Wald. There was no room for all of us together so the family was split just for the time being.

My room was small and on the ground floor of the house, but nice and clean and what I needed with a window at street level. From there, I could observe the main street with all the traffic and people passing by. I loved to sit at this windowsill for hours, knitting.

I learned knitting when I was seven years old in a little wool shop in Vienna from the owner, who seemed to like me. I became a good customer for years and probably that was her idea to teach me so every garment I knitted held my thoughts of my young life, my childhood rebuilt again and again. Most of all, of course, my thoughts directed to my love to Kuba.

I had lots of admirers in Vienna and Kraków, but Kuba was special, my first and only big love. Looking back more than sixty years later, I have found that you can be in love many times, but you really love only once.

10

MY HEART SKIPS A BEAT

It was a cold but sunny morning when I was sitting in my favourite spot at the windowsill and saw a man approaching Wald's house. Who could that be? Somehow the way he walked was familiar. I could not see the face straight away. He talked to the caretaker who was sweeping the footpath and pointed in the direction of my window. When the stranger turned towards me, I thought I was dreaming until he came closer to me and laughed straight into my face. I looked into his sparkling brown eyes, saw a bald head, a bit strange, but when I saw the set of beautiful white teeth, this remarkable smile, I knew it was real. It was Kuba who came after me, alive, safe and nothing changed besides his missing beautiful hair. I have been in shock; first I could not say a word. I did not jump or scream for joy. I sat where I was and could not take my eyes off of him!

So there he was. He had escaped captivity and gone through an ordeal to find me until he turned up in Lemberg, where he met our mutual friends. After all, I had left messages for him everywhere. I had been convinced all along that he would do anything to get in touch with me. Papa was thrilled to see him.

Now he trusted Kuba completely. Mutti and even my sister Susi pretended to be happy for me. For my sake only, he became a part of the family.

Papa finally had found accommodations for us all together. He rented a surgery from a retired dentist. After our long stay in the cellars cramped together without any privacy, we appreciated this new place. Kuba moved in with us and immediately took on all kinds of handyman jobs. He turned the surgery into a living room, the laboratory into a kitchen with a small gas cooker and the huge waiting room he divided into two bedrooms. Kuba himself slept on a sofa in the living room. I discovered his skills, talents and extreme tidiness, which I had never known before.

Our landlord was delighted and recommended him for many more jobs. We women decorated the place with old furniture given to us by relatives.

The Russians had taken all of our assets and money; there was absolutely nothing left for us. I think Herr Spanndorf still had saved a small amount of money from the country; as honest as he was, he handed it over to Papa. We had very little to start a new life with under such difficult circumstances. Nothing worried me as long as I had Kuba with me. He took any job available to keep us going. Papa, with his poor knowledge of Polish, had great difficulties finding a job.

Every business had been nationalized; the Communist regime had taken over everyone's life. We tried to hide the truth about our close relationship to the wealthiest family in town. We have been members of the bourgeois High Society for a change! It was as bad as being Jews under Hitler.

Susi went to High School to finish her matriculation. Papa's cousin's wife was a teacher there and tutored my sister and helped whenever she could. Susi was efficient, as she always was, and took her studies very seriously. She got a special permit to pass the final exams in German, with very good results.

I refused to go to school. I hated the thought of it. After all, I was engaged. It was not official yet, as we did not dare to trouble my parents, who had too much on their mind to cope with all the problems.

I wanted to contribute something, help Kuba as the present main provider in one way or another. One of our relative's sisters-in-law had a dressmaking salon and was lucky enough to keep it in private ownership. She offered me a job, the worst one I could have got, but I had no choice. The pay was lousy, as I had no experience.

Mrs Repper realised my "talent" right from the start and used me like a servant. So did all the other girls who worked for her. I was the youngest, and they all bossed me around, made me do all the dirty jobs like cleaning, scrubbing floors, picking up pins and needles, everything but sewing. I had to deliver suits, coats and heavy parcels to all their clients. Everything by foot, of course; there were no cars then or any other transport available. I did not complain about it at home, as it was better than doing nothing. I made more from tips for the deliveries than from my pay.

It was winter, up to minus thirty degrees. My hands were frozen even in fur gloves from carrying the bulky, heavy things. On one of those frosty days, when I was dragging along a fur-lined coat hanging in my arms I encountered my father. He was devastated; he had no idea how badly I was treated. He took the coat off me and carried it for me until we delivered it to the customer. Papa was always a real gentleman, who never raised his voice or got into an argument with anybody. For the first time in my entire life, he got into a rage. He walked me back to my workplace and went into the workshop, and in front of the girls, he screamed at the boss, abused her, called her names. I never expected those words coming out of his mouth. He told me to get my things, took my hand and got me out of there before I could even get a word in and have my say as well. He threatened to report her to the authorities, as she never cared to register me. The arrogant woman was so frightened that the same day she had delivered an envelope with the money that was owed to me for all the time I worked there.

It was quite an experience, and I learned my lesson to speak up for myself. Kuba could not believe that I went on that way for so long without telling him the truth.

It all contributed to my life experiences. I listened and learned from these common and uneducated girls, working at that place, Not only did my Polish vocabulary improve, but in particular I learned foul language, swears I had never heard before. I also learned about men, their attitude and demands on women and how to fight back. I hadn't learned about the trade, but rather how different people were. I heard about their upbringing, their reactions and generally about their lives. I developed a good common sense in recognizing their characters and most of all not to allow losing one's dignity. Now I hated this town with so many narrow-minded people even more.

After Susi finished her school, she took off to Lemberg to study languages. Her jealousy and attitude towards Kuba had made my life miserable. I was quite relieved when she left, and so I helped mother with the housework and learned to cook. I couldn't have had a better teacher. Mutti was such a terrific cook and always managed to dish up meals out of nothing. We started with Kuba to socialize; he met a lot of nice people at his job, where he had been in high demand. We went to cafes and dances as to private parties.

I didn't like parties. Wherever I went, I was the youngest. Most of our friends were married couples in their end twenties or thirties. I could never fit in. The drinking at parties, flirtations, kissing and cuddling and worse were new to me; I could never get used to it. Women were all over Kuba, as he was too good looking to keep him for myself. I wasn't interested in any other man, as innocent and inexperienced as I was. I felt so disgusted and disappointed. I went with him as I was afraid he would have gone on his own otherwise. Even worse!

On holidays in Zakopane with Józek, Elspeth and Eva. I am wearing a traditional Jacket of the Tatra Mountains' region.

I tried to get him more to the café dances than to parties. I loved to dance with my boy. Of course I liked to show him off as well. Mutti let me wear her fur coat or silver fox; both items she took with her from home, always well protected together with her jewellery. I did not have much to wear, but it did not matter, Kuba loved me the way I was.

We used to go always to the same café. Whenever we turned up, there was a man sitting at the same table. He was Kuba's age, tall, slim, good posture, but I did not like his face. He had a big nose and big ears. There was something strange about this man, I could not explain what, that made me stare at him. Always on his own, with a bottle of expensive wine in front of him, which he hardly touched?

The waiter filled his glass, but I never saw him drinking. I watched him out of curiosity. He got up and asked Kuba politely if I was permitted to dance with him? Kuba didn't mind, but I refused. He repeated his invitation every time we visited that place. He did this once every evening, always asking with impeccable manners. I kept refusing until Kuba asked him nicely not to try anymore as he annoyed me already.

I found out later about him from friends that he was a lazy womaniser who had never worked in his life. He was the only son in the family and his father's pride – why, nobody knew. At school, they called him the "Iron Student", as he repeated classes for a few years until he was finally expelled. His father tried to dig for oil without success and took his son with him to the mine.

One day, they both thought they are going to find *oil* and become rich, which never happened. His name was Manek Pomeranz. He came from the neighbouring town of Borysław, same town, where my family had their oil fields. I don't know why, but I could not get the man out of my mind, and we finally stopped going to that café, just because of him.

In the meantime, we had been warned that the Communist Party had started to dig further into our family's history and intended to deport its members to Russia. There were many people in the little town who had known us, most of all my former boss, who we could not trust. Time again to go into hiding. Kuba had been such a wonderful support to our family, Papa respected him and I had nearly turned seventeen. It was time to make our engagement official. My parents, of course, objected in the beginning due to my young age, but they could see how serious Kuba had been about me all along. It was a never-ending love story.

On 1 March 1940, we got officially engaged. We moved to a faraway suburb to disappear from watchful eyes. Bourgeois indeed! The place we got compared to the most primitive and uncomfortable living, right after the cellars. It was an old shop with one room and kitchen behind it. There was no running water inside, so we had to carry it in buckets from a well, five to seven minutes' walk. The toilet was outside with a tank, which we had to empty ourselves. When I look back, I am sure it was the worst dump I ever lived in. I could never come to terms with how my adored and wonderful Papa had to live in a place like this. Kuba and I were young and in love, so we didn't care, but poor Papa. I still get goose pimples when I think about it today!

Mutti got a job as a cook in a rehabilitation hospital in Truskawiec, a holiday resort. She worked terribly hard fourteen to fifteen hours a day but had her own nice room and plenty to eat for us. Papa visited her every week and returned home with bags of food. He, on the other hand, worked as a bookkeeper for several chain stores.

Kuba worked as a driver, employed by the Russian army. I stayed home all day on my own and kept house for my two men. Sounds lovely, doesn't it? I can honestly say I took a tremendous load on my shoulders. I had to carry water from the next well, which was ten minutes away from home. When carrying full buckets of water, it took me nearly half an hour. I placed a pole behind my neck sitting on my shoulders with the two buckets attached to chains on each side. I had to balance them and walk carefully, trying not to spill, as every drop counted. To pull the container full of water out of the well was already a job for a strong man. Before Kuba left for work, he got a big supply of water and filled up every available container, but it was never enough. I had to do our washing on a washing board in a big tub, after boiling it in a huge kettle on the kitchen hearth, fed constantly with wood.

My practical sense developed those days, at just seventeen years old. I used and reused this precious water for scrubbing the hard wooden floors, down on my knees with a hand brush. Then again this water I carried out to the "dunny" located outside at quite a distance. Also the dishwashing water was kept in a bowl on the side of the hearth.

The nearest shop could be reached at an hour's walk. Most of the time Papa and Kuba brought the groceries home. Most mornings I headed at 6 a.m. to the nearest market. Chickens were only sold alive. Either I was lucky enough to have them killed by the farmer, who sold them or brought them home clucking and fluttering in my shopping bag. Kuba was an expert in slaughtering poultry. I learned to cook, well equipped with Mutti's wonderful recipes and a helpful and patient neighbour, who taught me how to make noodles, dumplings (Placki karto-flane or potato fritters) and delicious yeast cakes. I walked in and out of her home to let her check on my newest cooking experiments. She was Ukrainian, and I learned many new expressions in that language, which helped me later in my times of disguise.

There wasn't even a war on, and we had to live without electricity, using kerosene lamps instead, without sewage, without water and worst of all, without a proper toilet.

What a fall from our once-luxurious life. I took it exceptionally easy. My biggest concern was for Papa to put up with all that. He never complained, but I could read him like a book. He always felt responsible for all of us.

As Jews under Germans or bourgeoisie under the Communist regime, we were the underdogs. We couldn't turn either way.

11

THE NEW
COMMUNIST REGIME

Kuba and I got married on 1 June 1940, six weeks after my seventeenth birthday. After endless discussions, I finally convinced my parents that my young age didn't make any difference. Kuba had proved his love and loyalty again and again, and as far as I was concerned, I had passed my test in coping with this hard life as well as a twenty-five-year-old would have. Papa's biggest concern was how the sex life would affect me. Mutti filled me in on all the details, including "faking". She was far more realistic.

As we left the Russian registry office, which was a simple formality with Papa being our witness and Mutti's wedding ring on my finger, I stepped into my new married life! I walked on clouds. I don't know if I was ever more proud or happy. All my life I couldn't wait to become older with every year. The main reason was that I always had to stay two years behind my sister. Suddenly I was well ahead of her, a married woman. We had no "proper "wedding; who could even think of a luxury like that? Mutti took a day off work and prepared at home a small celebration. Just for the four of us. After that, she lured Papa tastefully and diplomatically away from us to her place for a few days, so we could have our honeymoon alone. "Just be gentle with the child", was Papa's advice to Kuba. He of course didn't know that I had lost my virginity a while ago.

Love-making with Kuba was a big disappointment to both of us.

"So this is what it is all about?" I asked Kuba. I thought love-making was disgusting, but Kuba was understanding and gentle indeed. Papa didn't have to worry. Of course he was right: I wasn't ready yet. Aren't parents always right?

It didn't matter to me where I was and how I lived, as long as we stayed together. We were happy and in love. The "honeymoon" lasted no longer than two weeks. Another heavy blow struck us both. Kuba was forced to join the Soviet Army.

He disappeared for six weeks. I had no news and did not know if he was dead or alive. It was far too much for a seventeen-years-young bride. I got so depressed that I did not leave my home, only waiting for news, which finally arrived in the form of a nice young Russian soldier. He brought me a letter with the message that Kuba was heading towards Bessarabia (Rumania). It said that he was well and full of hope and good spirit and would be back soon. It certainly gave me my old optimistic spirit back.

It became a habit or rather an obsession to watch every military vehicle passing my windows or walking the streets to look out for Kuba's face.

Things sometimes in life really happen, when you put your mind to it. I was on my way to see my father's aunt, who had become a big support to me during these lonely, uncertain times living in isolation.

Aunt Henrietta was the sister of the now-famous movie director Robert Altman's grandfather, and she always told me never *to give up hope*. She loved us both, and as small as she was, she had such a strong and clever mind.

On this beautiful August day, I decided to take a long stroll to see her, watching as usual every passing military truck and car.

Suddenly a big truck loaded with Soviet soldiers stopped, and the driver waved to me, calling my name. He was wearing a Soviet uniform with a hat that covered his face, which I couldn't see. I walked slowly but did not approach the truck. Then he jumped out and ran as fast as he could into my arms, Kuba, my dearest Kuba, while all the soldiers were roaring and cheering to celebrate our reunion. He never looked better, although covered with dust and dirt from the long drive, He has been away ten weeks, but it seemed ten years to me.

After Kuba's discharge from the army, we moved to a better place at the Resort, where my mother worked.

I was definitely far too young and not ready for marriage. My mother had warned me and kept on telling me, how wrong it was to marry a man who was not only too old for me, but came from a completely different background. She tried to open my eyes, but I was blind. I thought she interfered in my life. My father, on the other hand, was far more tolerant and liked my husband, but he could see as well that I could not cope with the demands of a marriage, no matter how hard I tried. I was a child, and he was a grown man. I had no demands myself, but I had learned ever since I was a small child to fight back as far as it concerned my sister. I learned under her aggressiveness how to defend myself. When she hit me without a reason, I would hit back. I built a wall between us and protected myself from being her doormat. As much as I loved Kuba, I did not permit him to walk all over me either. I had a rebellious nature.

Today, after I have lived three-quarters of a century, I can see that marriages are only necessary to have children. You don't gain anything from being married. Having security, from what? You have to stay independent, rely only on yourself. As a child, you have to obey your parents, later at school your teachers, and when you join the workforce, your boss. In marriage, the husband wants to dominate you. I did not take orders, not even from him. The only person in my life I really respected, obeyed and looked up to was my father. He has been my greatest mentor.

In Berlin in my twenties.

Instead of slaving for a husband, I should have gone back to school and study. Unfortunately, it was the last thing on my mind then. Kuba was loving, caring and hardworking, but not a "Gentleman". He did not have the same upbringing as I did, he came from a small town and he seemed to speak a different language. I was far too young to adjust no matter how hard I tried. My love was not all I needed for the "real thing". Kuba had been adored and spoiled by women and had his affairs long before he met me, so he kept telling me in full detail. I had enough reasons to be jealous, and Mother perhaps put him down far more than he deserved. When we finally thought we had adjusted to each other and I began to cope better with married life, a big shock hit us once again.

In July 1941, another war between Germany and Russia broke out, and Hitler forced himself into the Russian part of Poland, pushing them out completely. Back to square one! No more "High Society" but "Bloody Jews", once again.

We moved back to the city, and Papa joined the Jewish Committee, which gave us some protection at the start. Now my great-grandparents' mansion, which had been occupied the Soviet Army, was taken over by the Germans. My ancestors would have turned in their grave knowing what became of this beautiful home.

12

Major Eberhard Helmrich

Papa's ability to speak fluent German helped tremendously in negotiations with the German authorities. Kuba helped him in arranging housing for the army and civil members of the government. He worked on renovations of the often very damaged and neglected apartments formerly occupied by Russians. That's where he met Major Eberhard Helmrich, who was the officer in charge of the food supply for the town. The Major, taken by Kuba's charm and skills, employed him as his personal assistant. Young Jewish women were forced together with men to register for all kind of odd and difficult jobs. Anyone who did not follow their order did not receive a food ration card.

Thanks to my own knowledge of German, I was assigned to the head of the Gestapo Obersturmführer Tolle as his house-keeper. Against all expectations, this *most feared man* treated me from the beginning with an unbelievable humanity. He did not see a "Jewish pig"; on the contrary, I was in his eyes a Viennese young woman who kept his home the way he wanted it. He protected my family and me. I even got his written permission *not to have to wear* the Jewish star. He walked me home at night to make sure I was safe. Otherwise he was very correct, never taking advantage of me as a woman.

Kuba organized a comfortable apartment with luxuries like a big bathroom, which we hadn't seen since we left Kraków. We moved in with my parents, and for a few months, we could live a normal life. I had two close friends, both married young sisters-in-law. They talked me into meeting one of their good friends, who desperately wanted to be introduced to me. I went along out of curiosity and perhaps partly to please them.

To my surprise and disappointment, it was Manek Pomeranz. He was none other than the funny man from the café, who kept on asking me to dance with him, and when I refused, was so inexplicably persistent. He knew I was happily married and wasn't the slightest bit interested in him. I did not even try to hide how I felt about him, ignoring him completely. I did not know then what a big part in my life he would play a few years later. You can change your mind about people, but the first impression I got about him was most of the time the right one.

13

ZWETSCHGENKNÖDEL FOR
THE HAUPTSTURMFÜHRER

I kept working for the Gestapo boss; he lived
in a three-story apartment house, where
he occupied the first floor for himself. The
remaining flats were occupied by his officers,
assistant and staff. A side wing was turned into
offices together with the interrogation chambers. From my boss's flat, I could look from a
window directly into one of these chambers.
What I saw and heard there haunted my nightmares for many years. I never saw my boss in
action, though; he had people who were happy
to do the dirty work for him – sadists, who just
got their thrills out of torturing Jews.

One of the sadists was an Austrian Sturmführer called
Landau. He was a drunken swine, sitting in the backyard of the
house next to his girlfriend "Trude", shooting at people with
his rifle like a bird hunter. He was so dangerous that nobody
dared to report him. I was so scared that I did not talk about
it to anybody. Landau was told one day that the big boss's
housekeeper came from his hometown, Vienna. He called me
into his flat with the command to clean it. I told him in my
best Viennese dialect that I could not take his order without
our bosses' permission. "Aren't you scared of me?" he asked,
astonished. "You know, I can shoot you"! "How would your boss

react", I replied, looking straight into his eyes, "if he would lose his housekeeper, the only one available who speaks your language"?

"By the way", I continued, "without his permission, I could get you some Viennese Zwetschgenknödel (plum dumplings), when I make some for the Obersturmführer"?

From then on, he became very friendly whenever I had the misfortune to meet him in the house. Was it my survival instinct or the anger and frustration that fought back? I never talked to anyone about how I felt or what I heard in this house. Not even at home did I mention anything, especially to Papa or Kuba, as I did not dare to alarm them.

There was one more incident with Sturmführer Landau.

One day, I heard him screaming downstairs on the ground floor. I ran out of the flat to see what was going on. A few petrified Jewish men were standing at the staircase, holding a broken chandelier in their hands with such agony in their faces that I could not help but to run to their rescue. The man who Landau assaulted, threatened and yelled at most was none other than my admirer Manek Pomeranz. I was sure Landau was about to kill him.

"I don't think, Herr Landau", I called over to him, "this ugly piece of a chandelier would have matched your elegant furniture. I will find out where you could get a much better one". He calmed down immediately and looked at me in disbelief. "Please, let the men go back to their work. The Obersturmführer sent me to see what the noise was all about?"

The Obersturmführer was not even at home that time. I just made that up, as nothing else could have helped more than mentioning the big boss's name. "Go to hell", he yelled at the men and disappeared into his flat.

Manek gave me a look like an injured dog, full of pain and devotion, embarrassment and admiration, as he got off the hook.

"You have just saved his life", one of the men said. "Manek dropped the chandelier and would have been executed". Landau never hesitated to kill when he felt like it.

God, I hated this man! I hated him and the whole bunch of psychopaths and murders at the Gestapo. Why, I kept asking myself again and again, had I been born as a Jew?

What was so terrible about *us* to be tortured and killed?

Papa became the most important liaison officer of the Judenrat (Jewish committee), thanks to his knowledge of the German language, his fairness and devotion to helping people. As a former member of the Freemasons Lodge back in Vienna, he had always been a fighter for human rights, a true gentleman by all means. That's why I always loved, adored and respected him more than anybody I have ever known. Kuba, who became the Major's right hand, supported Papa and the Judenrat when-ever he could; they made a good team. He introduced Papa to Major Helmrich, and they clicked immediately. They became the best of friends. Helmrich, as unbelievable as it sounds, watched more over the wellbeing of the Jewish community than over the Germans. He and my father had similar characters; they both constantly put their lives in danger to help others.

At that time we hadn't heard from my sister Susi, who still lived in Lemberg. We were all extremely worried and tried to contact her. Kuba asked the Major for help, and he immediately offered to go there himself to look for Susi. Two days later, he brought her back safe and sound, although she worried about us as much we did about her. He took her under his wings, giving her all the protection he could. He employed her as his live-in housekeeper. Under all these circumstances and uncertainties we came up on top, mostly thanks to the Major, who watched over us and was our "Guardian Angel".

Working at the Gestapo, though, it became almost unbear-able to witness their cruelty! My boss did not change his humanity towards me, but he did make it clear that whatever I should see or hear in the building had to be confidential – or else. I knew he meant it and kept my mouth shut. I tried to find a way to leave this place of horrors and torture, but that would have meant risking my life and those of my family. I could not leave "just like that". I had to have a good reason. As naive and optimistic as I was now at eighteen years old, I thought I had found the perfect solution. I wanted to get pregnant. I still can't understand how Kuba could have agreed to this crazy idea. Unfortunately he did, and it worked straight away. My parents were terrified, particularly my father. He knew exactly what was going on.

Every few weeks a new "Action" took place. The SS demanded a certain number of Jews deported to the camps. The Judenrat tried to protect them as well as they could, but the SS forced their way into homes of innocent people and dragged them out in the middle of the night.

I always thought with our protection nothing could happen to us. True, at the beginning, that had been the case. As long as I worked in his house, my boss warned me anytime an "Action" was planned. He even went as far as hiding my mother and me in his apartment whilst Papa and Kuba stayed at the Major's home with Susi. But even his protection could not last forever?

14

DIE ACTION – ON THE WAY TO CONCENTRATION CAMPS

The Action started by forcing people out of their homes like cattle from their yards. They were pushed into trucks and vans and brought into "Sammelstelle" (assembly centres). The "Ordnungsdienst", Jewish Police, had to keep them in place and make sure everything went smoothly, and everybody followed instructions. First the old, sick and disabled had to go, while younger people with working certificates were released.

Manek Pomeranz was a member of the OD (Ordnungsdienst). He disciplined thieves and crooks who committed burglaries and deception. They were locked up in cellars to protect them from the Gestapo. He became almost an expert in taking the law into his own hands. It wasn't an easy task for him, but somebody had to do the dirty job. Edek Galotti, a good friend of Papa and Kuba, was the head of the Ordnungsdienst. He and Manek were most of the time present at the Sammelstelle. They rescued hundreds of people from deportation. Some of them survived. But in return, he had to deliver a certain number of people to the SS. The locked-up thieves and crooks were taken instead!

Edek told us stories about the cruelty of the Gestapo and SS with the help of Poles and Ukrainians. Some of them were as cruel as the Nazis, obsessed with hate towards Jews. These stories were then hard to believe for people who just heard them. For me it was nothing new, as I have witnessed them for almost a year, working at the Gestapo quarters.

This is supposed to be the story of my life, not a historical report. So much has been written about it already. I don't want to repeat myself; it is painful enough to take my memories back to those most vulnerable times. So I will spare the details about murder, abuse and humiliation. When my pregnancy showed, Obersturmführer Tolle dismissed me from my job.

"You picked the worst time for having a baby", he told me. "I hope you won't regret it"! How right he was, how could I have let that happen? It wasn't an accident, as I kept telling everybody. It was the only way I knew to get out of hell!

Mutti suggested an abortion at the start of my pregnancy, but I wouldn't hear of it. I was so happy to have the baby, no matter what the consequences were. I was looking forwards to being a mother. I was so proud to carry Kuba's child. You could hardly see my face behind this big tummy. One day we went for a walk, my friend and I and Kuba with her partner behind us when I heard an older couple talking next to us: "If I could get my hands on that rascal", said the man to his wife in a loud and angry voice, "who made this poor child pregnant, I could strangle him". I pointed my finger back at Kuba: "My husband is the one, but please don't kill him", and everyone laughed. I looked so much younger than eighteen.

In the meantime Ghettos were being formed, more and more Jewish families were deported, separated or killed or just disappeared, gone into hiding. One member after another of my father's family were missing, among them Aunt Henrietta, whom I liked so much. There was also no trace whatsoever of my mother's parents. Helmrich asked one member of his loyal staff to investigate their whereabouts in Kraków.

This gentleman, called Paul Albers, Helmrich's secretary, brought bad news from the general government in Kraków instead. They did not select amongst Jews anymore; all had to be taken to Concentration Camps. It won't be long, he reported, before they were going to act the same way in our town. Helmrich had long talks with the Judenrat, most of all with Papa. He found the perfect solution to rescue at least a few hundred people. He found a big estate in order to establish a farm growing corn and vegetables, enough to feed the army of the town. Helmrich, an agriculturist, knew what he was doing. He proved to his superiors that such a farm was essential, and he got the approval to employ three hundred Jews. With this genius idea, the Major became the hero of us Jews. Helmrich was later recognized as one of the "Righteous Among the Nations" by Yad Vashem.

Kuba 1939

*The only man
I truly loved to
this day.*

He was a good-looking, tall, slim, blond, Germanic type – of elegant appearance. He was charming, and with his soft voice, he appealed to everybody, even to the Nazis. He was a perfect gentleman. Nobody ever saw him drinking; he would never take any bribes. Regarding women, he had his weakness as any other man his age. He was in his late thirties, away from home and his wife. He had the same wandering eyes as my beloved husband Kuba. Women were throwing themselves at him as they did with the Major. Helmrich was very discreet with his affairs, but Kuba wasn't. He flirted around whenever the occasion came along. My mother kept a close eye on him, and she saw much more than I did but didn't say anything to me.

Don't they always say that the wife gets to know last? I have been busy in the house Mutti prepared me for the birth and made sure I got plenty of exercise. I had to scrub the bathtub every morning and did all the cleaning to keep my body fit and flexible.

We got very close at that time. I could talk with Mutti freely about everything.

I was allergic to sex during my pregnancy, so I asked her about it. She had an explanation for everything and taught me how to pretend some interest. "If you reject him, you will lose him to another woman".

She also slowly prepared me to face facts about certain gossips, so as not to be caught by a sudden surprise. I saw Kuba very little during the day; he was so busy with the farm, like Papa, who was in charge of the workers.

I had some reliable friends working with him, and slowly, trying not to upset me, they told me what was going on there! Chyrawka, as the farm property was called, was situated on a hill. As I was far advanced in my pregnancy, I found it difficult to climb up there. But one day I made up my mind to see if all the gossip was true. I arrived at lunchtime, when the workers had their break. Most of them lived on site in small bungalows, flats or shelters. Papa had his office, which he usually shared with the leading staff. There were a few rooms attached. I was looking for Papa and Kuba and was told that Papa had just left to see the Major. As to Kuba, nobody apparently knew where he was. I could see some embarrassment in his friends' faces mixed with guilt and trepidation as I marched straight through the office across to one of the rooms. There was Kuba lying on a couch, facing the door, kissing and cuddling a girl called Hedda, who was my age. She was beautiful, and it was well known that she hardly could resist any man. I immediately saw the situation. I stood at the door laughing, ignoring completely what I had just witnessed. Hedda was so surprised that she immediately took off, running like mad. Kuba was lost for words.

"I came to pick you up, Darling", I said calmly. I was far too proud to make him a scene. I had to consider Papa's position as well. He, of course, like me had no idea. I took Kuba's arm, and we walked out of the office surrounded already by curious people, who were prepared to witness a fight. Far from it, I talked if nothing happened to everybody, joked, laughed and showed off my big tummy. I missed my profession; I should have been an actress!

Susi and her twenties in New York, USA.

15

A CHILD IS BORN

The birth of my first child was a piece of cake! Our bedroom was turned into a delivery room with a young midwife and an experienced older gynaecologist. Dr Gottlinger was a caring, fatherly type with whom I had had a good and friendly relationship since the early stage of my pregnancy. The most important and supportive person in this team was my mother. To have the husband at your side during birth was out of the question in those days. Mutti was at my side, holding my hand as she always used to when I was sick as a child. She prepared me for this birth and gave me strength and loving care as only a mother can give.

Giving birth to the first child is the most wonderful experience a woman could have in her life. For me it certainly was, despite all the pain. Whilst I worked so hard to finish the job, Kuba had started flirting outside with the midwife. She was not even good looking with a big nose, common looks and straight, dull hair. The only attractive part of her face was her big blue eyes. She responded positively to Kuba's advances and couldn't stop praising him even during my worse contractions. Mutti, with Dr Gottlinger's help, finally ordered her to stay in the room to see to her duties.

My sister Susi dropped in now and then with a frightened and worried face. She thought her baby sister was going through her worst agony. Just the contrary! I was so excited that I felt only half the pain. After three hours, a healthy big boy arrived weighing four kilograms. We called him Robert. Kuba and Papa were both so proud. Papa especially got terribly emotional becoming a grandfather. He was then forty-six years old.

Our happiness did not last long. Not only did I suffer big complications with my breasts, caused by producing too much milk, but we had to hide in Helmrich's house when a big "Aktion" was planned. The Major gave us a warning; just in time and with many other Jews, we went undercover in his cellar and roof loft. I had to feed the baby anytime he cried to make sure his crying would not give our hiding place away. My breasts were bleeding; an infection followed with high fever. The "Aktion" was one of the worst that happened in our town. Most of the Jewish families lost at least one or more members. People just disappeared, either taken by the Germans or they went somewhere into hiding. The Ordnungsdienst had the hardest job ever to keep these desperate people at the Sammelstelle under control. As Edek Galotti told us later, Manek Pomeranz had to watch his parents and older sister standing waiting for the transport. Slowly, in a well-organized way, he got out his mother and sister, step by step, carrying them on his back. His father, who suffered from *Basedoff* disease, caused by the thyroid gland, got so weak over the shock of the events and couldn't move. It was impossible to rescue him as well. Manek disappeared together with his mother and sister, and nobody knew where he was. Just in time, before the Germans could discover him.

When the terror was over, I had to undergo immediate surgery. Papa located the best Jewish surgeon in town, highly respected and protected by the Major.

Dr Sasza Weissmann was and, I can gladly say, probably still is a wonderful gentleman. Jews were not allowed to be admitted in any hospital. Sasza turned one of the rooms at the farmhouse of Chyrawka into a well-equipped theatre, where Dr Mischel, a general practitioner and father of my good friend Halina, assisted with the anaesthetic.

A trained midwife, Anita Brunnengraber, took over as the operating sister. It was a severe case of mastitis. Both breasts had to be operated on, and Sasza had difficulties controlling the amount of pus splashing out, which then caused ulcers all over my body. Even Anita, who instantly cleaned the abscesses, got infected and still has scars from that time, her lifetime souvenir, she says. After the operation, her devotion and care for the baby and me was so unique and sincere that we became best friends. When my parents came to see me in recovery on the operating table, Papa asked me if there was anything he could do for me? I said: "please promise me to look after Anita". He kept his promise in saving her life later on.

This friendship is still very much alive. She lives now in Berlin, and we have never stopped our friendship and trust in each other. She is one in a million.

Anita Brunnengraber (Birnbach) an Angel who cared for me after the horrific operation. My father in return saved her life later from the concentration camp. In the 1960ties she moved to Israel and had a good life with her family.

It took me a long time to recover from this operation; the pain lasted for weeks and far worse as the baby got infected too. There were no antibiotics available in Poland until 1946. The ulcers spread to the baby, Kuba and my mother and whoever came into close contact with me got infected. Sasza tried some radiotherapy in a small dose. He controlled the infection, but my nerves were shattered. The scars on my breasts were deep and long, and I was terribly concerned if they would show up in the future?

"It is entirely up to you, Darling", he said. "When you don't show them, they won't be seen". I took his advice seriously, and all my life I tried to hide my breasts. The scars are still there, after fifty-eight years, but the job was well done. I adored Sasza; this was more than a doctor-patient relationship. I had a big "crush" on him. He and his wife became good friends with Kuba, Papa and me. Sasza was at my side and comforted me when I lost the baby. My breast infection affected the child's whole digestive system right into the intestines.

Although baby Robert was under the best care of a paediatrician, our general practitioner and Anita, the best of all nurses, he could not be saved. I did not blame anybody but myself. I felt terribly guilty feeding him with already infected milk. I shouldn't have listened to the stupid midwife, who tried to convince me, even forced me to keep on breastfeeding. With my mother's instinct, I should have known that he was in danger. I was in a stage beyond consolation. Kuba and my parents were heartbroken. When I looked at my mother, I could hear her saying "I told you so". She didn't say it, but I knew what she was thinking. She had tried to talk me into an abortion, and I had refused. One thing I was then and still am absolutely sure about is that I never regretted having this baby, even though it lasted only six weeks. God knows what He is doing! They all said He had His reason to take him away.

It wasn't the first time already then, when I doubted, if there really was a God? Something died in me together with my baby.

I did not care, whether I would live or die! It made me harder. I took life like it came, day by day.

After rain, the sun shines again. Well, the sun arrived just in time to get me out of my depression. Helmrich's wife came to visit for the first time from Berlin. Already the day after her arrival, she came to see us, accompanied by the Major. I had seen him as somebody like a big movie star, a hero; he became just an ordinary, good-looking man next to her, nothing more or less. Her looks and her personality, the sparkle and warmth were overwhelming. The moment she walked into the room, she enchanted all of us. Helmrich must have told her my story as she sat down next to me, holding my hand. She came straight to the point. "We worked out a plan, the Major and I", she explained, "to save you women from any more hardship".

Due to the shortage of men in the war years, women were forced to take over their jobs. The German government made an allowance to bring in some foreigners to take over the housework for families. Ukrainians were the privileged and German-friendly nation who filled those positions.

"The Major", Frau Helmrich continued, "will see to it, that all three of you (Mutti, Susi and I) will get the necessary documents". Mutti refused to go to Berlin; it would have been too far away from Papa. Susi had nothing to lose, and I didn't care either way, not even about Kuba! One thing I knew: I wanted to start a new life and forget my tragedy. Donata Helmrich took Susi with her as she returned home. From now on, my sister was Helena Baranska, called Hasha, of Ukrainian nationality. As simple as that! Helmrich found a place for Mutti with one of his German colleagues in a neighbourhood town, where nobody knew her, as his housekeeper.

I went last. My birth certificate was under the name of Theodosia Pankiw, born 1919 (instead of 1923) in Bialystok, nationality Ukrainian.

My second husband Józek in a Polish Uniform.
He saved his mother and both sisters from the
concentration camp. Carried them out on his back,
risking his own life and they lived in the woods for
two years. His father was too weak to go
and couldn't be saved.

16
Life Undercover in Berlin

On a cold night in November 1942, accompanied by Helmrich's most trusted secretary, Paul Albers, I was driven by car to Kraków to catch a train from Drohobycz to Berlin. After a heartbreaking, tearful "good-bye" from Papa and Kuba, I started my new life undercover.

Wrapped in a huge red scarf covering me down to my hips, I travelled with an old servant-like suitcase. Paul Albers placed me in a corner of a third-class train compartment. He travelled first class. We pretended not to know each other. He was there, just in case, to watch over me. I covered my face with the scarf, pretending to be asleep. I let my tears go freely, holding back the sobs so as not to be noticed. Besides my birth certificate I had a document, a working permit as a Fremdarbeiter for Berlin, Germany, issued by the German Government in Poland. Everything was legal, stamped, signed and sealed. I slipped into my new identity with such self-confidence and without any fear of being discovered.

On the other hand, my heart was bleeding from leaving my parents and Kuba. I can still see them so clearly today, standing on the doorstep: Papa with his small, pale face with the tears running from his big brown eyes.

It was the last time I would see him in my life.

Kuba was standing next to him in his red jumper with his arm over Papa's shoulder to support him. They had each other, I thought; at least I hadn't abandoned them completely. Of course I felt guilty, but both of them persuaded me to go, for their sake as for my own. I didn't leave only to save my own life; I left because I couldn't stay in that place anymore. I wanted to put it all behind me. The baby, the "Aktionen", the Gestapo and the whole town, everything I disliked so much. I knew I would never return there again and I never did. There was something else I was so desperate to shake off: my Jewish origins. I intended to leave that behind with my name, my childhood, and my youth. I thought about it during my whole journey, disguised as a peasant. Better to change into a servant with a made-up past, false name, bought from a Ukrainian woman whom I didn't know than to be a persecuted and humiliated Jewish underdog. I had no doubts about that for the time being. I could play that role and played it very well. As Papa said to me when he was holding me in his arms, saying our "Good-byes": "It won't be for long". Anything was better than being "the bloody Jew".

Another part of my love was gone, finished but never forgotten.

So Berlin, Adolf Hitler, with his real, common name, Schickelgruber, here I came into the lion's cave to have my last laugh!

From now on, there was only Tosha Pankiw. Tosha made a good impression at the interview with Frau Helmrich's friends, Dr and Mrs W. They lived in a beautiful two-story villa, a few streets away from the Helmrichs' home. Not many questions were asked, and I could start straight away. Dr W was a well-known scientist, a chemist with his laboratory in the basement of the house. It was a big house of twelve rooms with a large family. A well-organized household in which everybody had their duties. They were kind and friendly and welcomed Tosha into their home. She took her job very seriously, eager to learn to run such a household. At the beginning, Mrs W did the cooking herself with Tosha just giving her a hand, watching her prepare meals out of nothing. The food rationing was strict and far too short. "You are going to take over from me, when I go to hospital in a few months to have my baby", Frau Doctor explained. She was a young, good-looking blonde, always perfectly groomed and dressed. The manicured hands never showed a sign of all the work she used to do before Tosha arrived. Twice a week, a cleaning woman came for the whole day to do the hard cleaning work. Sister Inge, the nurse in uniform, took care of the delightful little two-year-old girl and was supposed to take over the care of the new baby.

I still had to undergo the legal procedure through a camp in Oranienburg, where all the foreign workers were checked, disinfected, deloused and examined by a doctor. One day more of humiliation, and I felt free. Dr W took me to Oranienburg himself to make sure they wouldn't keep me there longer than a day. We were squeezed into a small room, mostly Eastern "Arbeiterinnen", fat Russian women, along with some Polish, Turkish and Ukrainian. How I got away with that for over three years, I don't know. We had to wait naked for hours until we got our disinfected clothes back and were examined for head and body lice. I was hiding behind a fat Russian girl with an enormous bust, which she had to hold together with a string. My scars on my breasts were still very fresh; it had only been a few months since the operation. I covered them with my hands to avoid any questions.

I skipped the line up to the doctor, slipped straight into the queue of the "declared healthy" persons to get a certificate, which was issued by a supervisor. Dr W was nearby to take me to the office to get my permit to work in his household. I still was weak and sore, physically not yet ready. Frau Doctor never pushed me; she let me work out my time. She insisted on me taking a lunch break and lying down in the afternoon.

Dr W, nearly twenty years older than his wife, seemed an old grouch running from the lab to the house in his office, always in a hurry, pretending to be busy and overworked. Maybe he was. Tosha didn't like him much at the start, and she tried to stay as far away from him as she could. "Don't take any notice of Vati", his teenage daughter from his previous marriage told her, noticing Tosha's insecurity, "he is not as bad as he looks; he just likes everybody to be on the go, as he is".

When the bitter December cold in Berlin started, the villa was covered with a deep snow blanket reaching nearly the door-step. Tosha heard a shovelling noise, which came from the side of the front door. It was early in the morning, but Tosh used to get up at dawn, being already fully dressed. She pulled up the heavy wooden blind of the large hall window to see where the noise came from. To her surprise, Dr W stood in front of the door with a big old hat and woollen gloves and shovelled the snow to clear the entrance. Tosha ran into the basement, found another shovel in the cellar next to the central heating stove, slipped into her long Polish boots and put her mittens on. After a friendly "Good morning, Herr Doctor", she joined in without another word. So side by side, they cleared the way. It was a beautiful morning, cold but as soon as the sun came out, the snow glittered in different colours, and Tosha got warm from all the effort. "Your cheeks are red like our apples from the garden", Doctor W noticed. "It's good of you to help. Run along and make us some hot coffee, my own bean coffee, you earned yourself a cup", he said. After a while, they both were sitting at the kitchen table with red noses over their hot cups, and for the first time since Tosha had arrived, Dr W talked to her in such a friendly way that she could not believe it was the same person.

"Your hands are very small and delicate", he said, watching her whilst she was pouring more coffee into his cup. "You are not born to be a maid", he said. "I certainly don't intend to become one", she responded without blushing. "I just wanted to learn proper housework and needed a change. There is a war going on; soldiers fight at the front and we civilians should do our share. Women are running the home front, so why not help the way we *can* as well?"

"I am so pleased you think like that, we certainly are lucky to have you in our house". Tosha got him around. It doesn't take much to fool them, she thought; just find the right words at the right time. He was nice, she thought. It takes a while to get to know people, how they really are. She was Tosha now all right, but aware all the time not to make the slightest mistake to give "Hansi" away.

She knew there would be questions waiting for quick answers. So there was no use playing stupid. Just stick to the story she had made up with Hasha, alias Susi. They were cousins; they had to consider their resemblance as sisters. Both were orphans brought up partly in Austria by an Austrian foster mother, who married a Ukrainian engineer in Poland. That explained the perfect knowledge of the German language. Their foster parents were intelligent, educated people who had insisted on good schools. The cousins were close, so they decided to come together to Berlin. They spent every free day together, one visiting the other. Hasha worked for an older couple in the film town of Babelsberg, in a suburb, which was forty-five minutes journey by the S-bahn from Herrstrasse Station.

These two were never so close to each other than in those three years of living undercover. They shared this big secret, the same fears, the uncertainty, what could happen back home to their parents? For Susi, it was better to live more isolated as she looked far more Semitic than I. Although she thoroughly plugged her thick eyebrows into a thin line, she could not hide the big nose and dark eyes, and to tint her hair blond would just have drawn more attention. She had a typical Jewish figure, overweight with wide hips, not anymore the attractive girl she used to be as a teenager. It was the first time she had not been any competition whatsoever for me, her younger sister; on the contrary, she was far worse off with this old couple, being so lonely, so I suddenly became her best friend.

Susi had always been physically stronger, but mentally full of anxiety, insecure and pessimistic. I always have been the opposite: small and fragile, but strong-willed, sure of myself, that I could do anything *really* put mind to. I believed in people and took them as they were. I had an easy-going nature, never worried about anything. I went through life with an open mind. "Happy, go lucky", so to speak, but sensitive and emotional. Some of my characteristic qualities changed drastically as I became older and full of experiences, good and bad ones. A few things, though, we both had in common: we were both survivors, and we could adjust immediately to any situation in our lives. We were both modest in our personal demands, compassionate and always ready to help people in need. We never neglected ourselves, as taught by our mother: "The most important attribute for a girl is her appearance". All those qualities we still keep even now in our seventies; we will always be proud of our upbringing by our beloved parents. The character "Tosha" was a little bit of everything in Hansi and common sense of an instinct for survival. Tosha was much stronger, more ruthless, shifty and observant. She took charge of Hansi's weaknesses; she never allowed anyone to look into her heart and soul. Not even Hasha knew what really was going on emotionally.

In the privacy of her nice, little bedroom, when she retired early at night, she was not anymore the disciplined, ambitious and hard-working maid. There was Hansi, tortured and depressed by the memories of her baby. She could have saved him, the baby and herself and taken the boy with her. The family W was so fond of her; they would have permitted the baby to stay in their house. Every single night I cried myself to sleep. How was I going to cope when Frau Doctor came home soon with the newborn? I was so afraid; it would open the wound, which had not healed yet. I missed Kuba and Papa terribly, and thoughts of Mutti all alone were tearing me apart. Yet in the morning, Tosha took over, and all nightmares were gone. It's true what they say, that time heals all the wounds. Tosha was too busy to think about "Hansi". A few months after her arrival in Berlin, Frau Doctor gave birth to a baby boy. He was his mother's and the nurses' responsibility. Tosha stayed away from him as far as she could. She practiced her useful talent in trading goods, as she had previously in the war, as for money you could only strictly buy your rations.

Dr W travelled a lot and had the best connections with Switzerland, the only neutral country in Europe that was not involved in the war. He brought or had sent from there Bohnenkaffee (coffee beans), the most missed article in Berlin's households. We had plenty of cocoa, chocolate, sardines and tins of ham and meat, which we had well-hidden and locked up. Our milk supply for two babies, nursing mother and Dr W, who suffered from anaemia, got extra rations and was sufficient, but not enough for trading in other food. Every morning the milk cart "Bolle" announced his arrival with the loud sound of a bell. He stopped at different corners at different times. Our turn was very early in the morning. I rushed with an already prepared thermos of wonderful-smelling coffee to be his first customer. The driver was an older, typical good-hearted Berliner with a unique sense of humour and a personality of his own. Every morning in return for the coffee, I got some extra milk without stamps. Those leftover stamps, I traded in at the market's butcher, served always by a nice Oma (grandma) who had taken over the stall when her son had joined the army. I tried to offer her some of my milk stamps, and it all worked without a problem. Sometimes I offered and brought her a bag of Bohnenkaffee or a block of chocolate, which I had to drag out from my boss explaining what wonders they could do for our dinner table. The meat supply improved remarkably in our household with some lard or bacon. No wonder my cooking was so much more appreciated than Frau Doctor's.

Good mood, affection, love, all that has always been the source of tasty, hearty meal. "Liebe geht durch den Magen" (love comes from a filled stomach) – an old but very wise saying. Tosha became so popular in the family, almost irreplaceable. Dr W trusted her completely, and when she asked for those valuable items to exchange them for essential food, he didn't argue any more. Though other people were starving and undernourished, his family couldn't have been better off. The exchange trade extended soon in much more than milk and meat products. The delicatessen next to the underground station "Neu Westend" supplied her with margarine, oil and sometimes even butter in exchange for alcohol from the lab or simple medication like painkillers or sleeping tablets, of which Dr W had a big supply in his medical cupboard. Tosha's trading business flourished.

Her Berliner dialect improved quickly. As she became friendly and close with the daughter of her boss "Ilse", she picked up this kind of German, very different from the Austrian dialect. Ilse, who wasn't very fond of her stepmother, like most of the children of divorced families, had been desperate for an older sister. She could confide in Tosha, came for advice and opened up about the failures of her own mother.

Tosha soon had been told all the family secrets and gossip. Everything helped to put all bits and pieces together about them, their characters and their habits. The more she knew, the better she could handle them. Ilse showed her around, and thanks to her, Tosha got to know Berlin, this once-famous metropolitan city like Vienna, Paris and London. The city after the bombing wasn't the same anymore. Kurfürstendamm, like the Viennese Kärntner Strasse, did not sparkle anymore with nightlife and luxurious shops and theatres. The big hotels like "Eden" disappeared. Cafes and nightclubs had been bombed to the ground. The Hotel Adlon was still there and a few cinemas. With a good tip for the waiter, you could still get a small table at the Adlon's cafe and some nice cakes without the food coupons. Ilse had shown me the first steps back into real life without hiding. She had been my umbrella under which I had been covered safely. There was a war on, no doubt, it wasn't a normal life, and it wasn't safe either. Yet the war affected every one of them, not only us Jews.

I was free to walk the streets without wearing the Jewish star.

Whenever Hasha and Tosha had their "days off", they went to the movies. I haven't forgotten the names of the famous actresses and actors of the forties: Kristina Soderbann, called the "Wasserleiche" (water corpse) as she drowned herself in every movie; Zarah Leander with her throaty voice singing: "Ich bin von Kopf bus Fuss auf Liebe angestellt"; Marika Rökk with "In der Nacht ist der Mensch nicht gern alleine" (Nobody likes to be alone at night); my favourite actor, Theo Lingen; the always dry-humoured butler, Heinz Rühmann.

When I survive this war, I promised my sister, I will make sure to see as many movies as I can. I remember they played Beethoven's Ninth Symphony at the start of every Wochenschau (newsreel) prior to a movie. I remember the hits: "Im Leben geht alles vorüber, nach jedem September folgt wieder der Mai (Everything passes, comes to an end, after every September follows another month of May). On and on I went singing these songs, as Lily Marlene or another of my favourites: Die Lore and die Lone and die Liese, das sind drei bunte Blümelein. I loved music, songs; I loved life, never intended to give up and never stopped fighting for it.

I could breathe the fresh spring air, watch the blossom of the cherry trees in our garden and enjoy sitting in the sun on my afternoon breaks.

It was spring 1943 when Donata Helmrich called me on the phone, asking me to come and see her, as she had a big surprise for me. She sounded excited and happy, so it must have been something good. We avoided seeing each other for our mutual advantage. You couldn't be careful enough! I ran as fast as I could along the beautiful tree-lined alleys, where their elegant villas still luckily not ruined by bombs. When I turned into the Westendallee, my heart was beating from excitement to hear the good news. Was the war going to be over? Well, let's find out. Before I decided to ring the doorbell, the door opened and I was pulled inside. Here she was standing in front of me, still wrapped in the same scarf as I had been disguised in on my trip to Berlin, laughing and crying at the same time. I thought I was dreaming, and I had to pinch us both to make sure it was real.

"Anita, is that really you?" I called again and again, hugging and kissing her. Papa kept his word. With the Major's help, he sent her to Donata, another life saved. I couldn't stay long, but a few hours later, after I had finished my work, I came back to hear all the news about my family.

They all were alive but far from safe!

The farm camp had to be closed. The Major offered to take Papa to Hungary where the Resistance was very strong and the Jews were able to get to America from there. Papa refused; he still had a small group of workers left on the farm that he had to look after, and Kuba was also amongst them.

Somebody had reported my mother being Jewish and hiding under false documents. She had been deported to a camp called Płaszów before the Major could intervene. This was another reason Papa didn't want to leave.

Kuba had had his affairs, Anita told me, "Don't worry about him". It did not come as a surprise. I had known about that long time before, but it still hurt. It had spoiled my good memories, killed my big first love and all my trust in him. Don't ever underestimate a mother's instinct and advice! My mother had been so right about him. She never did like him and warned me often enough.

There was no hate either! One more chapter in my life had ended. Tosha took over for good.

Anita's name was now Marysia Kulczycka. She went to Hamburg to work as a maid in lawyer's household. It was a nice home in Blankenese, an elegant suburb of Hamburg. Marysia soon became friendly with a young telephonist, who let us talk for hours without charge at night. To get even an interstate connection during the war was very difficult.

As Joseph Goebbels declared TOTAL WAR in February 1943, the bomb attacks became more and more persistent. Air raid sirens sounded during the night, people had little or hardly any sleep and the attacks interrupted and changed the whole routine of the household. The baby and his small sister were sent to the country with the nurse to stay at the property of their grandparents. Ilse's brother, eighteen, the only member of the family Tosha didn't like, had to join the army. Thank goodness for that, she thought, one mouth less to feed. The whole family despised the Nazis with the exception of the eldest son. As a member of the Hitlerjugend, he had been well brainwashed and trained to become a Nazi, a big disappointment and embarrassment to his father.

With the small children out of their way and Tosha running the house, Frau Doctor became bored with life, her always-busy husband and all the problems connected with war. Tosha noticed a big change in her. She disappeared for hours, and when she finally turned up, she acted strangely: withdrawn, restless or just sitting in her bedroom staring out of the window. More out of concern than curiosity, Tosha asked her if something was troubling her. "Is it my fault?" she asked. "Are you angry with me"? "No, no", Frau Doctor assured her, "it has nothing to do with you, if you really want to know. I will tell you my secret: I am in love". Oh!

That kind of confidence in Tosha was the last thing she had expected to hear. She didn't answer, just looked at her more amused than shocked. It made them both laugh! Then Frau Doctor started to talk, pouring her heart out, telling her the whole story about her gynaecologist with whom she had an affair. "I am going to need your help, you have to back me up", she whispered, although nobody could hear us.

"What do you want me to do?" Tosha knew how important it was to become her boss's confidant.

"I am going away for a few days, officially to see the children. Make sure my husband is not going to surprise me and follow". Don't worry, Tosha assured, that's easy, I will find an excuse to keep him here, just leave a contact phone number, so I can warn you, if necessary. "I know can rely on you. I will make it up to you, you'll see". That was all Tosha wanted to hear. Everything worked out fine; Dr W never had any suspicion whatsoever or intention to follow her. Ilse was the one who watched her stepmother carefully. Already as a child, her own mother had betrayed her father. Ilse would never forget that, she confessed to Tosha a while ago, when she had told her the whole sad story. Now she asked all kinds of questions and Tosha had to be very alert with convincing answers. She kept her going, helped her with her homework for school, especially with English, and as time permitted, they both went out to see movies.

During Ilse's summer vacation, they took the S-train to the bathing beach Wannsee, still untouched by bomb attacks at that time. Ilse couldn't believe what a good swimmer Tosha had been, and at night during supper kept going on about it. "Well", her stepmother remarked, "there are many more good qualities about our Tosha you haven't noticed yet". Their eyes met; they understood each other perfectly.

At the end of the year, the air raids became worse each time, extended during the day as well. Tosha tried to stay in the house with a comfortable and well-air raid shelter equipped with bunk beds, water and food supply. Everything prepared to survive for a few days. Her exchange trade still running with big profits, and she usually went on her shopping sprees after the "all clear" alarm. These restless nights were followed by the hard work of removing glass and dust after heavy air attacks.

Air mines, illuminated by searchlights called "Christmas trees", with their whistling noise were still worse than bombing. Amazingly, Tosha was never really afraid of being killed by these attacks. She believed so confidently in her survival that death had been the last thing on her mind.

All she ever wanted from all her heart was the war to be over. Every morning, pulling up the heavy wooden blind, opening the curtains and *blackout* windows, she listened to the street noises, the passing cars, heavy tanks and military trucks with soldiers from the "Flack" (air force or defence) in long convoys. One morning, she thought, I won't hear all that, the day will come when everything will stop, nothing but one big silence. That will be a sign that the war is going to be over (yet a long way to go!). Don't they always say that when you put your mind to it, everything can happen?

There were days of despair and hope as well.

One day we heard on the radio about a bomb attack directed at Hitler and his quarters. "That's it", I thought, and my heart was beating madly. I was so sure Hitler would be killed. This thought gave me so much hope. It didn't last long, when the second radio announcement came. Hitler survived the attempt on his life, receiving only light injuries, but four other people were killed and General von Stauffenberg, an aristocrat, had been arrested! So again, the devil remained unharmed, and all my hopes were shattered again.

Early one afternoon, Tosha was ironing Ilse's clothes when Frau Doctor came into the kitchen, all dressed up for going out in an especially good mood. She looked so glamorous, her blond hair set as usual as if straight from the hairdresser, her finger-nails freshly painted, in a gorgeous outfit matching her fur coat.

"Tosha, can you manage without me for a couple of days?"

"Don't I always, madam?" Tosha laughed at her. "Where are you off to?"

"Officially I am going to stay with my sister Trude, but between you and me", she explained, "I am taking a break from air raids to get a bit of a rest in the country". Dressed up like this? Tosha let her clearly know that Frau Doctor couldn't fool her.

"Well you know, I met this nice gentleman in my sister's house. He is on a few days leave, and he wants to take me out". Apparently he had a gorgeous little cottage in Neu-Ruppen with an unusual collection of paintings. So what else is new? Tosha thought but politely kept listening. Erika's big eyes were sparkling when she told Tosha about this wonderful, good-looking, elegant new lover. Obviously she had to talk to someone about him, she apologised. Her mother and sister were both so old-fashioned, well, she couldn't tell them.

"But can I really trust you Tosha? You haven't disappointed me so far. That's why I confide in you, and now you have got me entirely in your hand".

Yes indeed, Tosha thought, now it is the right moment to confide in her as well. So I did at the spur of the moment and told her my whole real story. "I am not Tosha", I said without looking at her, folding up Ilse's blouse. I told her everything about my husband Kuba. The baby I had lost, the traumas, the tragedy of my life that started being born as a Jew in Vienna the same day as Adolf Hitler (Schickelgruber), 20 April. I still today hold him responsible for all the terrible losses of my past. He haunted me for years. My anxieties, my insecurities later on in life and my nervous problems are all related to Hitler and his persecutions.

"I am four years younger than Tosha", I explained, "not much older than your stepdaughter Ilse". Erika listened in absolute silence. After I had finished my story, she got up, took me into her arms, somehow relieved to know that we both had our dangerous secrets.

"Your secret is far worse than mine", she remarked. "I can lose my husband, my children and this luxurious life, but you, Tosha, can lose your life. Don't tell anybody about it, not Ilse, not my husband, your secret is safe with me" She went to the phone and cancelled her date. "I have to recover from the shock". She looked tired and went upstairs to lie down.

Later she came to help me to prepare supper. I cried in the kitchen re-living all the memories. She asked a lot of questions. I answered truthfully. "No more lies between us, Tosha, you have a friend you can always talk to!"

I had taken a hell of a risk, I realized, with my confession, although I have known about Erika's double life, cheating on her husband. I don't know why I did it, putting not only my life in danger, but Susi's and Donata Helmrich's as well. Erika kept her word, and I kept mine. From that day on, we knew we could trust each other, as we both were living lies, only with the difference that I had to survive these dangerous years and Erika did not want to give up her comfortable life with her husband. She was too young and beautiful to resist all the temptations. She desperately needed the excitement of a double life.

She even went so far to push Tosha into her husband's arms.

At New Year's Eve, Erika, who stayed most of the time with her children at her parent's estate in the country, came home to celebrate the New Year. Tosha, who had been accepted ever since the big confession as a member of the family, took part in the celebrations. There was plenty of food prepared by Tosha, and Dr W was generous in supplying drinks. Erika encouraged her husband and Tosha to dance together and made sure their glasses were always refilled. Tosha and Ilse were quickly tipsy; they were not used to alcohol. Ilse made some remarks about Tosha in her bathers making an impression on men at the Wannsee beach in summer. Her father wanted to hear more details and got quite amused. He started to flirt with Tosha, and she responded in a cheeky and provocative way. Erika disappeared to make a phone call to her lover, and Ilse fell asleep on the couch. Dr W and Tosha ended up kissing until Tosha fell asleep on the couch. All she could remember was Dr W carrying her up the stairs and putting her into her bed. Nothing else happened; she woke up next morning fully dressed, and only her shoes were removed standing neatly next to her bed.

Everything was back to normal next day. Only Ilse didn't stop teasing Tosha, how she must have broken her father's heart. She wished her father would continue paying attention to Tosha, just to get back at her stepmother. What she didn't know was that Erika would be pleased about it. It was deemed to be only a New Year's episode under the influence of alcohol. They all were far too occupied with the horror of the increasing destruction of Berlin and other big cities in Germany. The air raids were announced at short intervals; there was hardly time to reach the shelter. The cellars were not safe enough, and people were buried underneath. Dr W started to prepare an underground shelter in the garden. Both he and Tosha dug together for days, and it was hard work. Tosha, so strong and young, was more than willing to help, as it was for her safety as well.

Dr W, pleased with all the efforts Tosha put in, asked her into his study at night for a drink. Life was so uncertain those days that you never knew what could happen to you next day, even the next hour. They thus took advantage of the opportunity to take what was left from something, what you could call a "living".

I can't tell you today, if it was "falling in love" or just an attraction to each other. Dr W was twenty-five years older than Tosha. She probably saw in him a fatherly figure, a protector who cared for her. She was flattered to get so much attention from a man like him. Dr W was a well-educated and respected man. Both were lonely, and they became lovers, backed up by Ilse, who was clever and shifty enough to find out soon what was going on. It didn't take long for Tosha to confide in him as well about her past. He was far less shocked than his wife. He knew all along, he said. Tosha must have had a secret, and she wasn't the Ukrainian servant she pretended to be.

Erika, who always took care more of herself and her children than of her husband, preferred to stay in the country with no intention or desire of returning to Berlin. She was much safer with her parents. So the three of us stuck together during those days of horror, between craters, ruins, rubble and smoke. The streets were full of injured people, dead bodies, starved, screaming and exhausted homeless people searching for some remains of their belongings.

Without exaggeration, it was hell – cruel and burning hell.

My sister kept in touch as often as she could. She got a new job with a colonel and his wife, as the old couple fled to some relatives in the country. The colonel was away most of the time, and Hasha and her lady became quite close. Only Hasha was more careful than her sister and did not confide in anybody. After every raid, Donata came running to see if we were still alive. Sometimes Tosha went to see her, always with a bag of food. Their house was among the few undamaged ones, and so was ours, until one evening when without any previous air raid warning, a severe bomb attack started. We just managed to reach the shelter in the house, too late to run into the "bunker" (shelter) in the backyard. The bombs roared, rustled, grenade attacks followed in such speedy intervals, that we thought the whole world was falling apart.

The house started to tremble, swaying like a ship on high seas. We heard the clatter of broken windows and rumbling of walls. We were sitting all three of us close together, holding each other's hands. Dr W, a tall, strong man, lost his nerve. He was frightened and trembled, holding his hysterical screaming daughter in his arms.

All I thought was that with this attack they must have killed Hitler. That was the end of the war. Not for one minute did I think, I could die! Not if so many bad Germans got now what they deserved! Why should I lose my life? I had survived so far; there was no way something could or would happen to me. I worried about my sister, about Donata, but deep down I knew that they all would survive as well.

I was first to get out, after the worst of all the air attacks I had ever experienced stopped. I ran up the stairs and could smell smoke and heard the rustling of a fire. I saw the flame coming from the rooftop. I ran to the loft, grabbed the prepared hose, but there was no water coming out. We had some buckets with water lined up and containers with sand. First I shovelled the sand into the flame, which was not too high yet and easy to put out. Then I poured buckets of water over it, until it stopped burning. Dr W finally dragged himself out of the shelter to look for the damage, I heard him scream and there he stood in front of a collapsed wall of his bedroom the whole corner of the roof was ripped off. At least the house was still standing, all the other rooms full of dust and rubble, broken glass but besides this one room, the roof and all the windows, the rest of the house was undamaged. We found a big bomb crater in the backyard, but our "Bunker "was untouched. Berlin had been destroyed completely. People were made homeless, starving and injured, and had no medication to keep them alive. Doctors and nurses were serving on the front lines. There were shortages of everything. The SS came doorknocking, desperate to take away the remaining males between 16–65 years of age. Ilse and I persuaded Dr W to hide and not follow these orders. It was his last-minute rescue. Of course men of the Volkssturm came looking for him, but we convinced them that he had not returned from one of his "war important" trips to Switzerland. He managed to get away to join his wife and children in the country together with his daughter Ilse.

I stayed on my own in the big house until my sister turned up to my surprise and delight. We both spent the last days in the bunker until the Russians arrived. Finally my long-awaited dream came true: The war was over!

17

THE WAR IS OVER!

Hitler disappeared, Goebbels and his wife murdered their six children and then committed suicide.

Our house was without windows, the entrance door broken; everybody could get in and do what they would like. Some Russian soldiers tried to get hold of us and steal some of the valuables, but Susi with a helmet on her head and big kitchen knife chased them away talking Russian to them. After we showed them our Ukrainian IDs, they backed off. One young Kierkese soldier tried to rape me, but when I started to cry, he took out a big handkerchief, smelling from cheap perfume and onions and dried my tears and let me go.

We were so lucky! A Jewish Sergeant, who had listened to our unusual disguise, took charge and protected us for the first and worst week. He stayed with us and supplied us with food and documents to secure us from any further harassment.

I picked up my old "trading business" and hitchhiked on a truck to go to the country to look for Dr W's family. It was a German driver and escaped soldier who offered to drive me there. We agreed to the price of a few bottles of liqueur.

He sounded trustworthy, taking a big chance. About halfway through our drive in the middle of nowhere, he raped me! I knew there was no way out – the Russians everywhere, no escape. That was the last humiliation I ever experienced with a German. I never told anybody about it, not even my sister.

He took me safely to my destination, but I refused to go back to Berlin with him. I joined a transport of German refugees back home. That was it; I didn't want to stay in this country longer than I had to. My romance with Dr W was forgotten, far behind me.

At one of my trading activities at the Brandenburg Tor, I met a Russian officer, good-looking, wearing a uniform. He stared at me, came towards me and said in Polish: "I'll be dammed, if you are not the Altmann girl, married to Kuba!" Oh my God, I thought, I have seen this face before. I realized he was none other than Manek Pomeranz, the mysterious admirer from Drohobycz! He was the first person from "home" I had met since the war was over. We hugged and kissed, and there was an emotional reunion between us.

I took him back into the villa, and we talked all night. He knew Kuba was alive, but he had no news about our parents. Kuba's parents were taken away in one of the "actions" and didn't survive. Kuba apparently survived the Płaszów camp (where Oskar Schindler had operated), where to my knowledge my mother stayed as well. Manek changed his name to Józek Werner and served as a lieutenant in the Russian Army. I listened fascinated to his story, which seemed like a fairy tale.

After his father had been deported, he managed as a member of the OP (Jewish security officer) to rescue his mother, sister and his girlfriend. They hid in the woods, where they dug a trench in the ground for their shelter. They lived there for eighteen months like animals. At night, they took turns finding food, which they exchanged for their remaining jewellery. The three women fought all the time; it was a living hell. Józek was nearly caught a couple of times on his food hunts, but was lucky to escape. He left the three women when the war ended and joined the Russian army. He came to Berlin, the centre of goods and exchange with plenty of valuable items. He stayed a few days and promised to come back and take me to Poland to find out about my husband and parents. In the meantime, both Susi and I lived an active life with English officers who were stationed at the Villa next door. They supplied us with a lot of food, coffee, soap and all the necessities. We were out of our minds from joy that now all the ordeals were over. The first day the war ended, Susi and I got so drunk that we were lying under the table and didn't crawl out until the next morning with hangovers that I still remember after fifty-four years. Donata, our guardian angel, came to check on us and tried to bring us back to reality. There was no holding us back; it was like being in a trance. We had lived through all the frustration, the humiliation and the lies, so we wanted to let go and enjoy our freedom at long last. Nothing could hold us back, not our good upbringing or our background. We jumped into every opportunity life had to offer.

In the meantime, Dr W returned with his family from the country; they were all one big family. Erika came to her senses for the time being at least, and Dr W seemed the caring husband. I did not care one little bit about him anymore or about any other German man. The short episode between him and Tosha just did not exist, as Tosha did not exist anymore.

I buried her documents in the garden. I don't know why. I just did it; I wanted her out of my life. They showed Susi and I their gratitude for saving their house, their belongings still there as they had left them, thanks to us. They had been good to me, and I had paid them back. We still could stay in their house, but I didn't work for them anymore.

Life had so much more to offer, only we never had realized it until now.

May 1945 was one of those gorgeous spring times in Berlin. So many years of our young life were lost, so we tried to get it all back, what we had lost in those five years.

Helmrich came back to us with no news about our family. There was no sign of life from Kuba, who was supposed to contact me at Donata's address. It was our agreement that I would not move anywhere until he turned up. Nothing!

Józek Werner, though, returned as promised with a woman's uniform of the Russian army, a big coat (far too long for me) and a hat. He also had some new documents to take me back to Poland to find my husband. He masterminded this trip in a perfectly organized way. Trains were always stacked full, and Germans were not allowed to travel out of their country. They were thrown out of all parts of Europe. In a word: chaos! As an officer of the Russian Army, Józek took every advantage he could get, and we travelled in the conductor's own compartment all night without any problems. So here I was again in Poland.

I thought I'd pick up where I left off in 1938 in Kraków. Wrong again! Freedom? Maybe from the Nazis only, from being the Jewish underdog. I didn't have to hide anymore, but under the Russian regime, we were far from free. Once you got there, you couldn't get out again, The "Iron Curtain" had been drawn to the free, Western world.

My search for my family started in Kraków. I did not know where to begin. I went to all the old cafes with the hope of meeting some familiar faces, old friends who survived, most of all to find Kuba with a message from my parents. It didn't take long to learn the truth. I met some friends from Drohobycz, one nice young woman, Klara Rubinstein, who had worked with me at the Gestapo. She survived the Płaszów camp and had been rescued by Schindler; so had Kuba. Thanks to a woman who worked for Schindler, he was lucky enough to be on Schindler's list. He had lived with this woman in the camp. Now I got the picture. He owed her his life and stayed with her. That's why I hadn't heard from him. I understood, of course. I was hurt, but in a way, I was happy he was alive. Klara had kept up a friendship with my mother in Płaszów. Her life was hell there. I think the details about her got blocked out of my memory, as they were too painful. All I remember from Clara's story was that Mutti had been transferred to the concentration camp in Stutthof. There apparently she had been killed with many others by drowning. I never wanted to hear more details about her death. As to Papa took his own life when he was taken to the Gestapo in Drohobycz. As the captain of his "sinking" ship, he never tried to save himself. He stayed with the few people who were left until they got him. I was so desperate, devastated after I heard all this news bit by bit that I didn't know where to go or what to do.

I felt lucky to have Józek, who stood by me and supported me whenever he could. He was very much in love with me, and this love went back to the time he met me, when I was married to Kuba. Remember that I had also saved him from the rage of the Gestapo man.

I did not want to go back to my husband! It was fate, it meant to be. I was angry with him that he didn't try to save my parents. I have forgiven him all the other women, but not the terrible loss of my mother. Klara told me that my mother always had the feeling that she wouldn't survive. She told her and a few others who got out of this hell, that when by any chance they would meet me, to let me know that she begged me not to return to Kuba. I respected her wish (I knew she was right); I did not even try to contact him. He was looking for me, as I heard later, but it was too late!

I left in a hurry with the encouragement of Józek, who tried to keep me away from him. Of course he didn't want me to meet Kuba, being so vulnerable; he was able to manipulate me. He was so good to me, that I really thought for a while that I loved him as well. I couldn't go back to Berlin to be with my sister Susi. I had no documents, no identity and no desire to face the Germans again. Józek went back a couple of times with a fur coat for Susi we acquired in Warsaw and a few other things she could use there. He also brought her the news about our parents. She, on the other hand, had no intention of going back to Poland. What for? She was so right!

Józek and I enjoying a walk while on leave from the Polish army.

With Józek still in the Russian army, we started our life in Warsaw. He got a good position as an officer in charge of the petrol supply for the army. Warsaw, like Berlin, was completely destroyed, especially the inner city, one big ruin. Some of the outer suburbs were still unharmed, and that was also where we were lucky enough to find a room. Amazingly the Poles were able to organize enough food and the black market was booming, but other essentials were hard to get, petrol in particular! Józek, shifty as he was, took advantage of his position. He could get anything in exchange for petrol. What he did and how he did it, I didn't know, he never told me. All I knew was that he had always a lot of money; we were never short of anything. Perhaps, I thought with my everlasting optimism, times have really changed for me.

My life, though, still wasn't in order. I had no identity, no legal name, any documents to prove who I really was. Kuba's wife, definitely not! Hansi Altmann sounded so Jewish, and the Poles still blamed Jews for all their misery, the war, their losses, not to mention the long German occupation. Anti-Semitism flourished in Poland more than ever. We couldn't get married, as I had not divorced Kuba. Whenever I tried to contact him, Józek used all his tricks to make it impossible. He got hold of Kuba's letters and destroyed them. I wasn't to know about it until years later. As soon as Kuba had found out that I was alive and back in Poland, he broke up with his girlfriend. Apparently he had told her all along that he intended to come back to me. I had no idea, but I would not have had him back anyway. I respected my mother's last wish!

During my short stay in Kraków, after I came back from Berlin, I looked up an aunt. Miraculously, she lived still at the same address. She had married my great-uncle, my paternal Grandmother's oldest brother. He was a well-respected gentleman and the head of the family. Aunt Gusti was Christian, which caused an uproar in the family. Twenty years his junior, she tried hard to hold her position. My mother was the first family member to make her welcome, and they became good friends. Even as a Christian, she couldn't save her husband's life. He got deported to Theresienstadt, where he was killed. Our reunion was very emotional. She was the only relative I was able to find.

My mother's parents, I found out, were starved to death after being forced into the Jewish Ghetto. I had had my doubts about their survival, but once confronted with the truth, it knocked me out. It was hard to comprehend that Grandpa, my old understanding friend, who had been such a support to me, had to end up that way.

Auntie Gusti and I wrote to each other regularly. One day I received her telegram saying to come to Kraków without delay, great news was waiting for me. I left immediately, and what a surprise indeed! My mother's sister Genia, with her husband Gutek and daughter Ala, had come back from Russia. Apparently they had been back for a while already, but hadn't thought about Gusti until Gutek met them accidentally on the street, as they lived near each other. They had changed their surnames too, as had so many other Jews; now they called themselves Krajewsky. My uncle was a clever lawyer who finally acquired some documents for me under their name, Joanna Maria Krajewska. "You never know", he said, "one day, you might need a father and my name". My real first name was Johanna. I have no words to describe my joy to have found some family. We never stopped talking; they had no idea what had happened to us. Unfortunately for me – not for them – they were on their way to immigrate to Brazil to a relative who was a millionaire.

Józek had a servant, a soldier, a kind of a "footman" or "orderly", called Jósef as well. So I had to put up with two Jósefs; I called him Josh. He was very devoted to his lieutenant and even more to me. He came from the country with no education, being narrow-minded but good-natured and willing to learn. He did the housework; I was teaching him to cook, do the washing and he always accompanied me – three steps behind me, when I went out shopping. He even followed me to the dentist, when

I had to have a tooth extracted. Sitting in the waiting room, he heard me screaming as the dentist did his job without any local anaesthetic. He jumped into the surgery next to the dental chair ready to knock the dentist down. Fortunately the tooth had come out already, and I smiled at my rescuer. That stopped him from any further attempt to attack the poor dentist. With Josh at my side, I always felt safe.

Having survived the War, losing both parents and a precious child would my future be any easier?

PART 3
Life Amongst the Communists

Józek my second husband provided well for us in Poland.

18

ANOTHER NAME AND A NEW CHILD

Józek, who could get away himself, sent Josh after me to Kraków with his strict orders to bring me back home straight away! Józek was so jealous that he couldn't even stand the thought of me being with my loved ones. He wanted me all to himself without anybody else. Poor Josh had no luck as I refused to go back with him; I wanted to stay with them for a while because I had missed my family so much. Finally, after a few days I gave in, out of pity for this young, innocent soldier, who feared the worst from his boss. Joanna, "short" in Polish – Hanka Krajewska – came back at last with a new identity. Of course Józek changed it to Joanna Maria Werner (his name), born Krajewska. My birthdate and place of birth I kept were my own.

My next shock came when I learned I was pregnant. Józek always told me to be prepared that we could never have children. As a young boy, he had suffered from an inflammation of the testicles, and a doctor told him he would stay infertile. He was surprised but extremely happy to become a father. At that time, we occupied two simple ground floor flats without water and an outside toilet. Josh carried buckets from a nearby well, scrubbed the wooden floors and kept everything spotless. We both lived in one flat, he next door to us in the other. He was a tremendous help in those days but had no future with us. He wasn't used to such a good life.

To top it all off, I found out one day that he was wearing my underpants! Noticing that pink, silky fabric slipping out the back of his trousers, I asked him, pulling it out a bit further, what that was? He explained without hesitation, that his underwear was not as pleasant as mine was.

His stupidity was too much for me to tolerate. Despite all his good will, devotion and honesty, I was too afraid to trust him with a baby. He wanted to leave the army anyway, so Józek helped him to get discharged. He returned to his village, and we never heard from him again.

One day Józek's mother came to visit us, unannounced. She stormed into the house, followed by her eldest daughter, Nusia. From the first minute I met her, I disliked this woman. Nusia was better and quieter, and tried to be nice to me. They hadn't seen Józek since the war had ended; they hadn't spoken to each other for over a year.

I had a good friend, Marysia, who lived around the corner. Her husband was an officer as well. Józek and he were colleagues, and the four of us got along very well. Marysia organized the home for us when I got pregnant. She expected her baby two months before me. We both had a lot in common.

When I realized how Józek's mother had treated me in my own home – or at least I thought it was my home – I took off and ran to Marysia's. Józek came later with his sister to explain and take me back, which I firmly refused to do. I stayed with my friends until the bitch left after a few days.

Now I could understand why Józek never tried to keep in touch with his mother. By the way, he was as bossy as she was. It wasn't Józek's fault, but still it spoiled our relationship. How was I to know that it wouldn't happen again? Józek assured me that it wouldn't. Apparently he told her to leave, although she had come prepared to stay a couple of months! I tried to believe him, but I had seen him standing next to her, lost for words, embarrassed and humiliated like a child.

I came down with German measles when I was seven months pregnant. The doctor told me to stay in bed and rest. Either he didn't know, or generally in medicinal circles it wasn't known then, what danger my illness presented to the unborn baby. I had no idea! I recovered quickly, the baby was moving and everything seemed perfect.

I was looking forwards to becoming a mum again and hoped it would be a boy to replace my first one. Wrong! Once you lose a child, you can't replace it. The fourth of November 1946, I gave birth to a healthy boy, who we called Peter. He was born in the military hospital, where Marysia had also had her baby daughter. Everything went normally, only I missed my mother terribly. I remembered when I had had my first baby, how she surrounded me with so much love and care.

Peter was strong, and as the paediatrician assured me, a very healthy baby. I felt on the top of the world and so did his father. The home we had rented seemed comfortable, nicely furnished, the best we had had so far after my return to Poland. At least, we thought so. With a cold, long winter approaching, there was not one of the big tiled stoves in any room in a working condition.

We got the water into the house by an electric pump. It did not work either. We had to use the hand pump, which took more than one hour to pump the water supply for a few hours. I had to boil the hand-washed nappies in a big kettle on the kitchen stove. Nobody was even dreaming about a washing machine in those days, least of all in Poland.

Józek helped, but he was far from skilled in comparison to Kuba. He left in the morning for work and came back late in the afternoon, expecting everything to be done, cooked, ready to sit down, playing with his baby, who he was so proud of. The baby was good and quiet, but every newborn child has to have his moments. There were plenty of them that I had to cope with. I came from Berlin, after the best training for a house-wife. Everything had to be perfect, when it came to cleanliness, spotless and tidy. I learned a lot from Sister Inge, the baby's nurse: hygiene, regular feeding, daily baths and especially how to prevent nappy rashes. The conditions they had had in Berlin, despite the war, were so far different from the poor conditions were now in. As Józek lived in this underground hole for one and a half years previously, he thought now we were blessed with all the luxury he had lived without. We both had our points of view, but it did not work.

I was not strong enough physically or mentally. I had not come to terms yet with the terrible loss of my parents. Here I was, twenty-three years old with a lot of experiences, both good and bad, a good upbringing, but not prepared at all for a life like this! What I desperately needed was my mother. Oh God, how I missed her! No wonder my big joy becoming a mother again, the only wish and dream I had, since the loss of my first baby, had been spoiled by those hard living conditions. I insisted on following the paediatrician's advice on breastfeeding, which took a lot of my strength and caused constant tiredness.

Józek had not the slightest understanding. He adored the baby, but at the same time he was jealous that I devoted myself only to our child. True, all my love and attention went in that direction only. Józek's mother, delighted to hear about the arrival of her first and only grandson, demanded to see him. Well, I couldn't deny her that but dreaded her visit. At least we were prepared for it this time.

To my surprise, she made herself very useful. She was a great cook and prepared nourishing and delicious meals. As short and slim as she was, much smaller than I am, she had energy and strength. I had to admire her. She never took "no" for an answer. Her son, a tall, heavy man, not a bit like his mother in looks, had to do what she ordered. She gave him a talking to whenever she thought he needed it; and did he ever need it!

Surprisingly she joined forces with me, supported me, I think all for the sake of her grandson. I still didn't like her, but I had great respect for her. She was a devoted mother, in the first place to her daughters; her son, as she used to say, had been one big disappointment to her. As soon as we got to know each other, I understood why. She told me what he had been like as a child, the youngest and only son, spoiled by his father. Now and then I went back to these flashes, seeing him sitting for hours in the café, showing off with his bottle of wine he never touched. He skipped school for months without his mother knowing.

My mother-in-law and I made peace with each other – Mama, as he insisted I call her. From then on, she was always there when needed. She was fair and supportive, but for me too distant, too different from my family to even to make any attempts to love her. I was grateful for her support, but I never saw a mother in her.

19

A Heart Is Broken Again

When little Piotruś, as we called him, Peter in Polish, was three months old, I realized a sudden change in him. From his usual nap, he woke up suddenly with a terrible scream. It was nothing like the normal baby scream, rather a sharp long roar. When I lifted him up, it was gone. He rolled his head from one side to the other, lying on his back and didn't stop until I put him on his tummy. He was such a strong baby otherwise, lifted his head straight, like he was trying to sit up. He had a gorgeous smile that warmed my heart.

With the freezing conditions of February and the temperature dropping more than minus twenty degrees Celsius, I came down with the flu. Józek stayed at home and looked after both of us. He tried hard, but it wasn't enough, given what the baby was used to and needed. I was still breastfeeding him, but with the experience I had with my first baby, who caught my breast infection, I was too scared to continue.

We consulted the female paediatrician who had looked after him ever since he had been born. She advised me to collect my breast milk into a bottle and avoid any close contact. Marysia sent us an older, experienced woman named Tomczykowa, who had raised half a dozen children of her own. She not only had a lot of experience, but she was used to hard work.

During the day, we all were well looked after, but at night I still had to get up in this icy cold room. We had only a small iron stove, which had to be fired with wood constantly. The baby slept in his father's bed to keep him warm. He woke up during the night and had to be changed. Although I always used a mask around my face as a precaution, I couldn't prevent the baby from catching my cold.

He got very sick, with a high fever and a bad cough. The doctor visited every day and assured me that it was only bronchitis, which wasn't unusual for babies his age. The medication she prescribed didn't seem to be helping. The fever stayed on. I suggested getting him to hospital, but the doctor was very much against it. I couldn't understand why. I discussed his sudden continuous screams and the tossing of the head with her. As she couldn't find any ear infection, she explained the screams as a nightmare, not uncommon for babies. I trusted her, I believed her.

Yet, one night, when Piotruś couldn't breathe and got blue in his face, we rushed him to hospital. We got him another well-known paediatrician who confirmed what they told us already at the hospital: that he had contracted pneumonia. It was late February 1947, the year penicillin was introduced to Poland. They started to treat him with injections, which brought the fever down. I stayed day and night, as long as I could with him. The Catholic sisters from the hospital "Of the Saint Kopernik" were terrific. They organized a private room for me next to the hospital with a Polish family. I slept only a few hours in between pumping my milk for the baby.

I hadn't recovered from the flu, and the sister at the hospital, listening to my cough, warned me to take precautions, see a doctor and not to get pneumonia myself. All I cared for was my little boy. After a short improvement, he deteriorated.

The matron suggested that the baby be baptized. We had always put it off! Józek insisted that we never admit we were Jewish, but deep in my heart I still believed in God, our God. Baptizing the baby did not occur to me, and Józek didn't care. I was hanging onto my last straw. Perhaps baptizing would answer my prayers? Which God, whose God was the real one? I was terribly confused.

The matron with all her experience knew that the child couldn't survive. "Let him die in peace". I had seen the expression in my child's eyes. The same lost look I had seen on my first baby! I never, ever can forget that look, accompanied by a silent groan. I couldn't accept the truth! He was on his way to Heaven.

The following morning, a nun came to the family with whom I stayed with to inform me that Piotruś had passed away "peacefully". What did she really know? He was haemorrhaging from his ears, his mouth and bowel. Nobody, none of the doctors or specialists, could tell me what was really wrong with him. The pneumonia had been taken care of; it certainly didn't cause his death. They suspected meningitis.

I never stopped investigating, studying medical books and magazines. Many years later, I found out how German measles contracted by a pregnant woman could harm the baby. Or had it been an overdose of penicillin, which he might have been allergic to? All that happened half a century ago, and I still don't know the answers. It has haunted me all my life. It caused me great pain to write this chapter. I can never talk about it without bursting into tears.

Marysia was a wonderful support and devoted friend. I don't know how I would have survived this difficult time without her. My own health was also in a terrible state. My lungs were infected, I had a high fever and my nerves were shattered. Marysia took me into her home and nursed me until I got my strength back. She was like a sister to me. I was in no condition to attend the baby's s funeral, and Józek together with his mother blamed me for the baby's death. "You are not capable of raising children". She did and said everything to let me feel guilty and depressed.

If not for Marysia, who talked sense into me, who showed me compassion, I would have left Józek. I wish I would have been strong enough to do it then. My whole life would have turned out entirely differently.

Marysia had a baby girl, two months older than Piotruś, the worst and most difficult baby I have ever seen. Marysia was a perfect, extremely patient mother, but there were moments she wished this child had never been born. When my baby became ill, she told me later, she was praying to let her daughter die instead of my son. Marysia, like most Polish people, was a devoted Catholic and regular churchgoer. When Ivonka came down with a severe ear infection, Marysia thought that she had been punished by God. Of course she deeply regretted her prayers. But often she mentioned to me how unfair it was to lose such a precious child.

This time my faith and belief in God... died forever. I had always had my doubts, but now I was convinced that it wasn't "God" who could punish me so hard.

Józek stayed at home. I never asked why, as my grief together with my illness turned me to apathy. Finally I found out that he had been dismissed from the army. He was lucky that his boss, a Jewish major, covered up for him; otherwise he would have ended up in jail. There were too many officers and civilians involved in his illegal trade with petrol; somebody had to report him. It had been obvious it couldn't last.

We had to leave in a hurry, somewhere away from Warsaw, where nobody knew him. I did not care where we went; I had always been on the "run". I could have stayed behind; we weren't married, and nobody would have come looking for me. Yet, I couldn't leave him, as his grief was as big as mine. We had just lost our child; we had to stick together. He had been good to me; there was a moral bond, but no love from my side.

We had other good friends in Warsaw, Daniel and Nina. Both were Jewish and had been lucky to survive the war. Józek had met Daniel in the army, and his wife, much older than I, had taken me under her wing. "I wished", she always said to me, "my husband would love me as passionately as Józek loves you. You take it so cool without showing any emotion!"

She was the one who opened my eyes. I had taken him for granted. He was jealous, possessive, domineering; he wanted me exclusively for himself. Nine years older than I, he tried to manipulate me, my life, shut me off from everybody I ever cared about. All these characteristics turned me against him.

Thanks to Nina, I realized that his love for me made him like that. "At least try to pretend, be wise, don't turn him away"! It was too late; I couldn't leave him now. I should have remembered my first impression on meeting him in the café with Kuba. I had disliked this man then. What an unforgivable mistake I had made, falling into his trap at a time when I needed his help, being vulnerable and lonely back in Poland. It was my fault, not his.

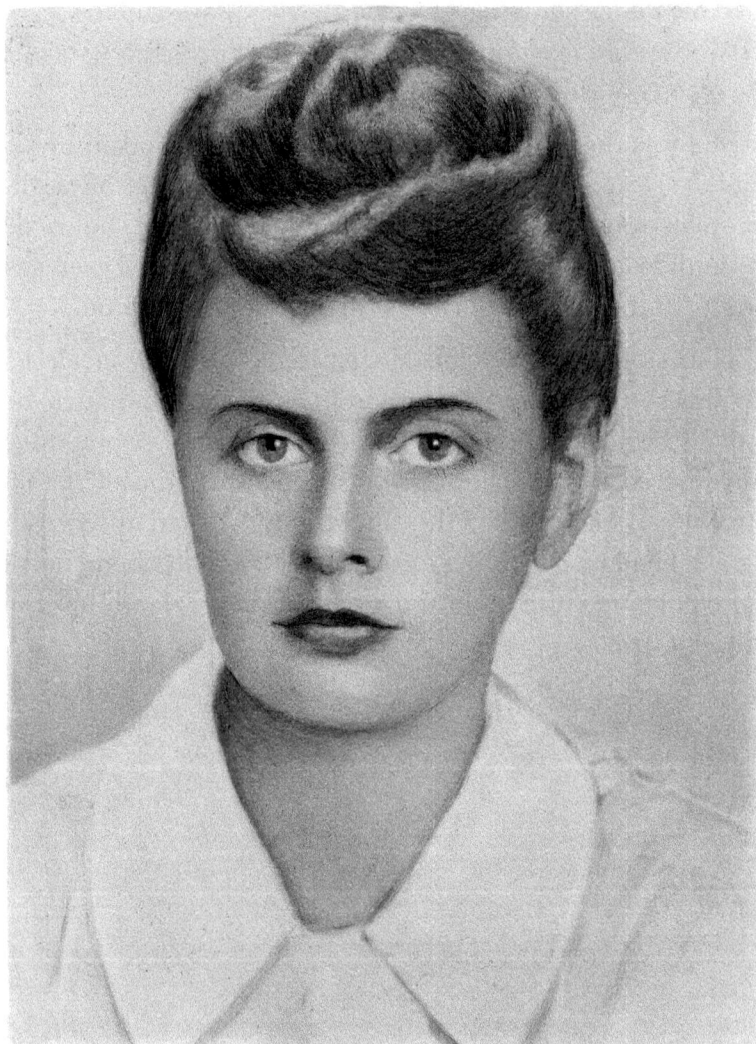

In Poland late 1940ties.

20

On the Road to Recovery

We arrived in May 1947 in Gdynia (Gotenhaven). I did not care where we went, what we did or who I was. I had not accepted that my second child had died. I acted strangely, talking and singing to the baby if he were still there. Most of the time I stayed by myself as Józek was busy making a living. I missed not only my baby, but my parents as well. Oh, did I miss them! I asked myself again and again the same question: "Why did I have to survive to come back to this kind of life?" We started all over again.

It was another rented room, but at least this time it was a nice, large one in a modern, comfortable flat. Our landlady, a divorcee, occupied the other three rooms with her two sons, who were ten and thirteen years old. She was a nice, intelligent lady, ten years older than I, and was the only person I had contact with. Józek liked that. All he ever wanted was to have me to himself – no friends, no relatives, entirely dependent on him. Gdynia was a nice small harbor town, next to Gdansk (as Danzig had been renamed) and the well-known holiday resort Zopot. You could still see a lot of the ruins left by the war, but it was a clean, pleasant town overlooking the sea. It fascinated me, as I have never lived so near to one. I used to sit on a bench staring at the sea for hours, daydreaming and pretending my baby was still alive!

On one of my strolls around the city, I met a good friend from the past, Halina Mischel. Her father was the doctor who had assisted my breast operation after the first child in Drohobycz. She had gone to school with my sister Susi, and they had matriculated together. We had befriended her and her boyfriend Mietek with Kuba.

Halina was on holiday with Mietek, now her husband, one of the few survivors from the past. They stayed in Zopot, and Halina came shopping to Gdynia. She knew I was living with Józek and that we had had a baby. I didn't tell her that little Peter had died. I couldn't admit that I had lost another one. She had attended the funeral of my first baby and was a great support to me then.

I told her that the baby was staying with Józek's mother for a while until we got settled in Gdynia. I talked to her like the baby was still alive, and I believed it myself. Was I going crazy?

I would have but with the help and support of "Pani Zosia", my landlady, who pulled me out of this deep depression. First, she tried to talk me into some activities. I couldn't work, as my knowledge of the Polish language was too poor. I had no profession. I wanted to do something, but I did not know where to start.

Zosia started to teach me Polish in a proper way. She supplied me with books about Polish literature and history. She opened a whole new world of Polish culture for me. I had always been interested and talented in foreign languages, and that was a start in the right direction. It kept me going slowly but surely so that I could face reality again.

Zosia was my only friend and adviser those days. She pulled me not only out of depression but talked me into trying once more to have another baby. The only cure to come to terms with our tragic loss would be one more child!

I took the bus to the nearby beautiful beach in Zopot, found a private spot there and did a lot of soul-searching. I had no ambitions, ability or motivation to build a business career. Józek never encouraged me; on the contrary, he degraded me, made me feel low and insecure. With the loss of my parents and the disappointment with Kuba, and without my sister or anybody close, I had lost all my self-confidence, had no demands whatsoever and led a simple life from one day to the next.

21

A BABY GIRL

A ll I wanted was a child I could raise in peace.
Once I made up my mind, it worked immediately. I became pregnant again: Józek was out
of sight and my control most of the day. I trusted
him when he told me about his good job as a
manager of a big chocolate wholesale company.
He was busy all day and let me believe he had
to work overtime at night. Finally, I became
suspicious and found out that he was gambling
most of the nights playing poker. This was a
side to him I never expected or known before.
It shows how little you know about a man, even
living with him for two years.

That was it. I packed my bag and took off to my good friend
Nina, who at the time lived in Łódź, in a palace of a Polish count,
previously occupied by a German SS leader. He had had to leave
everything behind when the Russians took over. Daniel, Nina's
husband – the one who had gotten Józek the petrol job – had been
transferred from Warsaw to take a high position in the Russian
Army, and he had been given the palace as his living quarters.
Nina kept inviting us, and finally, I took her up on her offer.

I appeared there unannounced one day and was received by
both of them like a member of their family. Nina looked after

me in her caring way. She was a clever, intelligent and ambitious lady. First, she tried to lift my self-confidence. She had wonderful taste and dressed me in elegant, modern maternity clothes. She again convinced me of Józek's love and devotion and gave me advice how to get him out of his gambling addiction.

I knew already then that I could never return his love. Yet I couldn't see a way out of this relationship, carrying his baby. I wanted a child more than anything in the world. In the end, Nina convinced me to go back to Józek.

My daughter Eva arrived two weeks late, but so quickly that I didn't make it to the hospital. Within one hour from the start of labour, she arrived in my own bed, with the help of a midwife whom Zosia found in a hurry. She was born, her head in a "bonnet", which according to our old superstition was supposed to bring luck. I believed it.

Now our life had to change. Józek, who left a big gambling debt behind, had to go into hiding. Once again, we had to move. It did not make any difference to me; I was so used to that kind of life. All I was concerned about was my baby being brought up in a healthy, comfortable environment. I learned to love the beach with the tranquillity of the sea and the white sands with the dunes to hide. That's where I wanted to bring up my daughter.

This time I had wanted so much a girl, as I had been convinced that boys were dying on me. I was lucky, as Eva was my first girl. Her father was as crazy about her as I was, and this brought us closer together. We decided to move to Słupsk, not far from the former German beach called Stolpmünde (in Polish, "Ustka"). Słupsk was a formerly German town, now taken over by the Polish government. Most of the German population had been thrown out of their homes or fled voluntarily, while Poles took their place. Only a small percentage of German farmhands and labourers lived in the countryside.

Józek was pleased with the choice of this small town. Not only was he safe from his creditors, but he could keep me away from my friends – the further, the better, making me more and more dependent on him. His jealousy was an obsession.

At this time of my life, I had only one goal: to keep this child alive. I didn't let her out of my sight for the first two years. I breastfed her for nine months as I thought that mother's milk was the only elixir of life, the only way to raise a healthy baby. This long time breastfeeding made me very weak and tired. I lost more and more weight and lost my teeth, and my blood pressure became far too low. If not for my doctor's persistence, I would have fed her another year.

Eva was toilet-trained exactly after one year. She started to walk at fourteen months, but spoke fluently when she was two years old. I talked to her constantly and never used baby talk. I read her stories, and she listened with delight to poems and ballads. Her memory was unusual, as was her ambition to learn. We grew inseparable.

Eva was the only person her father was not jealous of. He looked after us with great care and love, wrapped us in cotton wool and spoiled us. He got a perfect position as general manager of a major retail chain of the small town. As we lived under a Communist regime, he was employed by the government. We finally got a comfortable five-room apartment on a nice street close to the city centre. My health, though, did not improve much; I was weak and had all kinds of women's troubles. I desperately needed some home help.

Józek's mother, who often arrived unannounced, persuaded her son to get us a housekeeper. Elspeth arrived like an angel sent straight from heaven. One of Józek's employees, a German woman, introduced us to Elspeth.

My first impression of her wasn't too appealing. Dressed all in black, including her stockings, straight hair combed back in a knot. Clean, neat, but she had no personality. With such a bright child like Eva, I was afraid they wouldn't get on too well. She was that typical German country woman I had seen plenty of in the small town. Her severe looks, I thought, could be marks left from her difficult life. Her hands showed signs of hard, physical work.

During the interview, I found out that she had been assigned to hard labour in the fields. The Germans were treated badly by the Poles. To the Poles, the Germans were still the enemy who had to pay for all of Poland's hardships. Elspeth, who seemed very nervous, told me her life story in a few sentences. She used to work as a chambermaid and kitchenhand on the estate of a German count. She had learned the trade at the age of fourteen and worked up to the kitchen, until she took over from the old cook. She had been widowed during the war. She was not yet over the loss of her husband and of her home taken by the Poles, lowered from her position with an aristocratic family to a labourer in the fields.

She desperately wanted to get out of her village, where she was treated like a slave. I believed her and still remembering what I went through not long ago, I gave her a chance. She was in my eyes a human being, not a "German enemy". My intuition told me not to go by looks but rather to use common sense. I knew I could help her to change, get over her insecurity and feel at home.

For the next twenty years, she became a member of our family. I returned the favour I had received from the family in Berlin where I worked as a maid, the Jewish victim undercover. She became my friend and confidant, but never learned our Jewish background until many years later when we returned to Vienna.

Elspeth took over the household with efficiency I had never even dreamed about. I could trust her completely, and best of all, my precious girl got a second mother. Józek became a well-known personality in the little town. Establishing chain stores, one after the other, the retail business grew to such an extent that it had been noticed everywhere.

As the general manager, the Communist Party approached him again and again to become a member, without any success,

He refused to join them. He had become far too important in the trade to let him go, which he knew, and after a while, they left him alone. As the big boss, they called him "Panie Direktorze" (Mr Director). In Poland, as in Austria, the wife took her husband's title. I was addressed as "Pani Direktorowa", and Elspeth, who only spoke German, called me "Frau Direktor". I remained Frau Direktor for all the time we lived in Słupsk.

Although Józek accomplished a lot, his position went to his head. He walked around in a leather coat and hat, looking like a Gestapo man and feared like one. He had his staff well under control.

As he couldn't live without his game of cards, poker in particular, I let them play in our home to make sure it was kept under control. The games of cards went on till early morning hours but were quiet, as I made sure he invited men of good background and behaviour. I had to deal with some of their wives, though, who were against the long hours their husbands stayed away from home. To keep everybody happy, I invited the wives as well and organized a women's circle with a lot of fun and plenty of gossip. I could have never done all that without my Elspeth.

It helped me as well to fight all my depression and health problems. I was far from over the loss of my parents, grandparents and my babies. I missed my sister Susi, who had immigrated to New York in 1946/7. I had nobody! My mother's sister Genia immigrated with her family to Rio de Janeiro, to the other end of the world. We kept in touch; they sent me parcels, and so did Susi. She collected second-hand clothes from relatives and friends, in great demand in Poland. For Eva, she sent baby food through the "Care" organization, completely unknown and unavailable in Poland. Eva used to be the best-dressed little girl in town; so was her Mum.

Susi's life in New York was not easy either. She worked in a slimming parlour and later on as a housekeeper for a cranky, moody old father of one of our relatives. She had some on-and-off relationships until she finally met her husband David, to whom she got married in 1950, her best decision ever. After our Papa, David was one in a million, a man worthy of the most respect I have ever known.

At the age of three, Eva already spoke German fluently as well as Polish with Elspeth, who never even tried to learn Polish: "I am German and stay German". She always used to point out we spoke only German at home.

Eva was as difficult and stubborn as she was intelligent and eager to learn. Without any embarrassment, she got up in front of a large crowd at her father's staff parties and recited poems and ballads like "Pan Tadeusz" for fifteen minutes or longer without one mistake. She loved to be the centre of attention. When it wasn't a show, she made one up.

Playing poker with his friends, Józek kept Eva sitting on his knees, as he believed she would bring him good luck. When he lost, he sent her away, telling me that the child had had enough and she was tired. I tried without any success to keep her away from the gambling atmosphere, sitting in clouds of cigarette smoke until she fell asleep.

Elspeth adored Eva, but no matter how hard she tried, Eva always found a way to make her life difficult. She used to lift Elspeth's skirts in the middle of the street and showed to passersby what kind of knickers Elspeth was wearing. Poor Elspeth arrived home in tears, and Eva couldn't care less when she got punished. She made up stories and lies that were difficult not to believe. Elspeth, though, took everything with admirable patience. On her free days, she took Eva by train to the country to visit her parents and sister.

That was the only time this cheeky little monster turned into an angel. Elspeth was so proud that she could show off her wonderful girl to her family. They treated her there like a princess. Most of the time, I took Eva everywhere with me. In summer, we went to the nearby beach "Ustka", a half-an-hour train trip from home. We spent all day in the sun at the beach and played in the water. While she slept in her pusher, I enjoyed reading. Most of the time, Józek picked us up by car to take us home. One of those beautiful hot summer days I wore for the first time a swimsuit that Susi had sent me. It was made of a stretch material that was flattering for the figure, but not suitable for sunbathing. I was squeezed into this unusual material and could hardly breathe. I became sick, vomited and nearly fainted.

Eva, three years old then, did not hesitate to run to the road and arranged a horse and cart to give us a lift home. "My mum is dying", she explained to the driver, who immediately came to our rescue He placed me on some blankets on top of the carriage and Eva next to him on a high seat overlooking the whole street.

After a few minutes ride, she caught sight of her father's car. "Stop", she yelled to the driver and waved, standing on top of the seat. Fortunately Józek turned slowly towards the beach road, spotted her and stopped. I don't know what I would have done without my daughter's quick reaction? She organized everybody. This happened often enough that she did the right thing at the right time. I never wore that bathing suit again!

As we lived in that small town, everybody knew everyone. In particular, Józek was the focus of interest. The stores grew from one street to another, and more and more people were employed, so it was no wonder he became so well known. With his head up high, he walked around beaming with the confidence of a prime minister.

He was lucky to have been surrounded by experienced and well-trained people who ran his office. He himself had no idea about accounting, bookkeeping or any kind of office work. He couldn't even use a typewriter. But on the other hand, he was a terrific organizer who had a good nose for business and choosing the right people for the right job, but most of all a tremendous talent for bluffing everybody. With bluffing, he achieved whatever he wanted and left all to the professional work of his staff.

We made a lot of good friends among them, such as his first assistant and accountant Franek C. Franek was older than Józek and was a capable and intelligent man. He was the first and perhaps the only executive member who looked right through him and realized how little Józek was really educated. He shared this secret only with me.

Slowly I got to know what was going on in his office as I visited him every morning when I took Eva on a long walk. She used to sit in his office on top of his desk, chatting with everybody, making herself the centre of attention, as usual. Józek had a young, beautiful secretary, Cesia. She was bright and efficient, with such an appealing personality that Eva and I loved her from the moment we met. We became the best of friends; she came to visit us at home whenever she felt like it and adored Eva.

It did not take long, however, before I suspected that something was going on between her and Józek. I had found her sitting on top of his desk, with her sexy legs bouncing in front of his nose. When I entered his office unexpectedly, I was told by Franek that I "better keep an eye on them", so I just observed. Józek, of course, denied everything when I demanded an explanation.

I liked Cesia too much to get to the bottom of the matter, and Eva would never let her go; she was as enchanted by her as her father was. I just pretended to be blind. After a while, Cesia got involved with a handsome young man, a law student, far more appropriate than a happily married man her father's age.

Our friendship lasted without any hard feeling when she admitted one day that there had been a short affair between her and Józek. We were sunbathing at the beach; we were talking about her engagement to her new boyfriend when I popped the question: "Did you ever go to bed with Józek?" She admitted what I had suspected all along. She told me every detail, which helped me to see the other side of my loving, possessive, jealous husband.

Of course, I can't remember after all these years what I felt then. I know it was a shock. It made me furious, but I wasn't hurt. I did not blame Cesia; it had taken a lot of guts to admit her affair to me. She was young and flattered to have a relationship with the big boss. Not long ago I myself had been in the same situation with my boss in Berlin. He had been married as well; I didn't feel any scruples, as his wife had betrayed him for years. Cesia did feel guilty, particularly as we were good friends and stayed that way until she married and moved to another town.

From that time on, I became aware of his double life. At home, he was the loving husband and father, spoiling and protecting us. On the other side, he had his short affairs, jumping from one relationship to the other. I knew there was no love involved; even the sexual urge was not so important. It was mostly his ego, his vanity to prove to himself that he, suddenly *Number One* in this town, could have any woman he wanted. Once he had proved himself, he got bored and let it go again.

His women were jealous of each other and kept sending me anonymous messages. I found letters, typed or hand-printed, in my mailbox or slipped under the door telling me with whom he was having his present affair. Some of these letters I followed up and proved them right; some of them were made up.

I felt humiliated, of course. He was embarrassing me in front of all our friends, who knew and thought I had no idea. In those years, I played games with him, pretending I didn't know. But whatever feelings were left for this man were finished!

Wait, I thought, just wait. One day I will pay you back. But I never confronted him until much later.

I had a wonderful friend, Helena, with a young and good-looking husband; he was no different than Józek. Helena and I joined forces and confided in each other. She, like I, did not have to work and had a housekeeper looking after her two boys. She had a boyfriend and showed me the best way to pay a cheating husband back. I wasn't interested in other men then, not until many years later. She just injected ideas into my head, which took time to develop.

I covered up for her anytime she went away with her lover. We both spied on our husbands, and I have to admit we took a lot of pleasure in it – especially finding out what terrible characters they got mixed up with. Neither Józek nor Mietek were choosey at all.

I moved out of the bedroom and slept in my daughter's room, much to her delight. I refused any physical contact with Józek. The thought of sleeping with him made me really sick. I never told him why.

This situation went on for a long time, two or three years, until my dear Józek dug his own grave again. The personnel manager of his company was a woman, a Communist, an active, devoted party member. She had control over all the employees, she could sack people and she disliked without any explanation and employed whoever she wanted as well. She had more power in the company than even Józek. He always needed her approval concerning staff, a hard nut to crack. She was strong like a rock and made everybody's life miserable, the most feared and hated woman around.

Yet she had one great weakness and guess what? She fell deeply in love with Józek. It did not take long for my shifty husband to take advantage and get involved with her. Then and only then, he could wrap her around his little finger. Her devotion and love for him became even stronger than to her beloved Communist Party.

Helena and I observed this odd couple with satisfaction. Małgosia was as ugly as her character, much older than Józek, fat like a cow. Dressed always with the same clothes, a party badge on her big bosom, with dull hair tied back in a bun, she couldn't have looked worse!

Everybody in the office and in the stores, people all over town knew what was going on. I couldn't keep up my tactics under those circumstances and came out in the open. "What on earth", I confronted Józek, "do you see in this ugly bitch? Don't you realize you're becoming the laughingstock of the town?"

Of course he denied having an affair. He just pretended to be nice, he explained, for the sake of the company. He needed her; she could achieve everything with her connections, whatever he wasn't able to do himself!

Frank supported me and tried whatever he could to get him out of her claws. Too late! There was no way back. Finally Józek himself had had enough of her and started a new romance again with a pretty, young girl. Hallelujah!

We all thought he had gotten rid of the old girl, but she clung to him like a leech. One day, she turned up in our home, telling me about his romance with this young girl. To her biggest surprise mixed with disappointment, she got an entirely different reaction from me than what she had expected.

"I think they are a wonderful match, the two of them", I laughed in her face. "Józek is too handsome to waste his time with old and ugly women".

She left beaten with her "tail between her legs", and that was the last I heard from her. Not Józek, though. She used all her powers to have Józek sacked from his position. That was the end of our stay in Słupsk.

Once again, we had to move. Where to? Frank, our good, reliable friend, after long hours of negotiation with Helena, Mietek and another friendly couple came up with the idea to move to Poznań, formerly the German town of Posen. It was a much larger city, in which you could easily disappear. We all feared some further revenge from this woman.

I stuck by him all the way – not out of love or nobility, just sheer pity, loyalty and hope he had learned a lesson. All his affairs had meant nothing to him. They were the weakness of a man who missed out because of the war, as he went through hell to survive, a Jew haunted by Hitler, who had lost his identity, his moral values, everything he ever believed in.

We were similar creatures, sharing this secret of being Jewish. I, for my part, had lost much more. My only family was my daughter, whom I adored, and so did her father, whom she needed desperately. He would never let her or me go. He would have put up a fight for us, and I would have never been able to win, not at that stage of my life.

After all I had gone through with him, I knew him better than he knew himself. There was neither love nor hate. I was willing to start over again – stronger, harder, prepared to fight back. Once again, I lost count what time around we started another new life in Poznań.

Józek had changed indeed. Back to reality as just an ordinary man with a small family, no more the idolized big boss, he concentrated on making a new living. I have to give him that; he always made a big effort to care for us with his utmost protection. Our devoted, faithful housekeeper Elspeth joined us. She had already become a part of our family, and I could never have made it without her moral and physical support. I travelled a lot then, always carrying my bundle of joy, who never left my side.

We visited my friends Marysia and Nina in Warsaw, the city I loved most. With the help of those two ladies and Elspeth's admiration and support, I got my self-confidence back. I refused to take orders from Józek anymore; he couldn't stop me from going where and when I wanted to. I loved to go to the theatres with their wonderful performances.

The coffee shops in Warsaw had a specific atmosphere, unique to all other countries. They were always full of people, overcrowded at lunchtime until late afternoon. I loved to sit there observing people. Women in Warsaw had outstanding taste in clothes; they knew how to wear them, always groomed, keeping up fashion trends and hairstyles. They reminded me of my mother, who had the same qualities I learned from them. I became far more aware of my appearance, and with Nina's help, I found the touch I had been missing for so many years. I became confident and improved my knowledge of Polish, but always kept my Viennese accent, "Don't ever try to lose it", Nina preached,

"That's your individual charm". No matter how hard I would have tried, I couldn't have managed to get rid of it anyway.

I enjoyed these trips tremendously. In winter, we went skiing to Zakopane in the mountains and in summer to Zopot, where I felt already at home. Eva loved to sit with me at the international tennis tournaments for days; she never got bored chatting up people, who were delighted with her intelligence.

Józek met there a lady friend with whom he had had a short affair in the army. Although she was heavy, she was still good-looking and hospitable, full of life and wit. We became good friends; her husband was a plain, good-hearted customs officer. Janka shared Józek's interest in cards and organized partners for him to play every day. She had a son who was Eva's age; they became good friends, and I had my freedom to finally enjoy life.

22

FIGHT FOR LIFE

A nother blow of fate struck when we nearly lost our precious daughter at the age of six years. She was skipping with her rope together with her best friend Krysia when she suddenly felt a strong pain in her stomach. Elspeth and I got worried, as Eva never got really sick, besides her usual tonsillitis. I made her take some castor oil, which I remember used to be my mother's cure for children's stomach troubles.

It seemed to help, and Eva continued skipping. At night, though, she complained of more severe pain and was running a high fever. We lived in a rented house in an outer suburb of Poznań, only reached by train from the city. We had no car in those days and no taxis available. There was no hospital, and our local doctor did not answer the phone. The ambulance refused to take us, as stomach pains and fever was "nothing to worry about" for a six-year-old child. We kept the fever down with aspirin and compresses. I kept giving her enemas, another old-fashioned treatment for children in those days.

Finally, early the next morning, we reached our doctor, who called straight away. He diagnosed a strong attack of appendicitis and took her to the hospital.

Unfortunately it was a Sunday, first of May, a big Communist public holiday with one surgeon on duty in the hospital. He told us the appendix had ruptured, and the situation far too critical to operate. There was no way the child would survive.

When I heard this opinion, I froze, but my mind was still working. I became calm as never before. I didn't believe what this doctor just told me; I was absolutely convinced that my girl was going to live. I ran as fast as I could to the matron's office and barged in unannounced; in a few words, I explained to her that I couldn't stand to lose my third and only child. She understood and directed me to the best surgeon in town, Professor Dreffs, who could try to save her.

Józek jumped into taxi and drove to talk to him. He wasn't on duty that day and wasn't willing to operate on his day off. Józek went down on his knees, begging him to save his only child's life. He cried and screamed, and finally Professor D gave in. Józek collected the nurses from their homes, who assisted at the operation also in his taxi, and Eva was operated on immediately.

Only thanks to his skills and the antibiotics, the infection could be fought. We waited anxiously, Józek hysterical, I still calm and icy cold inside the waiting room, yet convinced I would get her back. When Professor D rushed out of the operating theatre, I chased after him to hear the verdict: "In three days, I will be able to tell you if your daughter is going to live!" was his comment when he finally decided to talk to us.

"Can I stay with her?" I asked.

"You will be a big help. She needs her mother", he approved, "but make sure her hysterical father stays away!"

Thanks to Józek's hysterics and his begging, Eva got her life back! She recovered quickly, but all the heavy drugs affected her mentally. For many months that followed Eva was sleepwalking and suffered from nightmares. I was fully aware that Józek was the one who saved her life, and so my heart reached out to him – once again!

Józek no doubt was a unique and remarkable man. He had a special way to impress people and make them respect and trust him. When he set his mind on something he wanted, he got it!

23
POLAND – A BEAUTIFUL COUNTRY

In 1954, cars were hard to get. New ones were available only to Communist Party members in high positions, doctors or police. The trade in used cars, spare parts and tyres in particular was flourishing.

Józek bought a rundown garage for a small amount of money, and with the help of an old expert, he built a business repairing and vulcanizing tyres and recapping wheels. The wheels came out good as new from his workshop, and it didn't take long for him to become the number one second-hand dealer in tyres in the whole town. He worked hard, got up early every morning and spent all day in his workshop. He learned the trade himself from his workman, who as skilled as he was with his hands, had no brains for business. The cash flow increased with every month. Józek concentrated only on his business and family. Twice a year, I went on a six-week holiday with Eva: to the beach in summer and skiing in winter.

Poland is a beautiful country, mainly valleys surrounded by the Baltic Sea in the north and Tatra Mountains in the south, the lake areas in the North West. This country is as versatile in its scenery as Austria; I would go even that far to say that it offers more in marvellous beaches and secluded dunes. As an adult, you see a country in a different light. You appreciate its beauty so much more as you learn about nature, which you ignore as a child or teenager.

I didn't like Poland when we lived in Vienna. All I saw were narrow-minded, old-fashioned people who seemed different from us, as I could not speak their language. As a teenager, when we fled from Hitler, the last thing on my mind was to explore the countryside. We were building a new life. I was busy making friends, and my social life was far more important. My first and perhaps only love started here in Kraków, and I was wrapped up in finding romance.

Although all the good and bad memories haunted me by visiting Kraków, where I had gone to see Auntie Gusti quite frequently, I loved this town in particular. Yet it had changed a lot. A new city had been built next to it – Nowa Huta. There were huge ironworks, steel construction and concrete-panelled factories, which spoiled the charm of historic Kraków.

In winter, I extended my trip to the nearby Tatra Mountains with its famous ski resort town Zakopane. It had the best ski conditions I have ever known. The slopes were easy to access by mountain railway to the most popular resort, Gubałówka, or further up by cable car to Kasprowy. As I had always feared heights, I never even tried those cable cars.

Gubałówka was what I enjoyed most, as did Eva. We hired sun chairs for the day supplied with blankets, which we hardly ever used, as the sun was so hot and strong. Everybody was sunbathing in sleeveless tops and bikinis. On the top of this mountain, it reached around twenty to twenty-five degrees, whilst down in Zakopane, the temperature was sometimes minus ten or minus fifteen degrees. In February and March, this sunbathing area was so crowded that by noon you couldn't get a sun chair anymore. We always came early enough to find a good spot. The country women, dressed in their traditional clothes, colourful and beautiful costumes, carried around big metal cans with hot milk and baskets full of fresh blackberries and small strawberries, which they topped up with fresh cream.

They belonged to this wonderful, characteristic place like the snow, the sun and the whole scenery.

It was absolute heaven up there. I liked skiing but was not mad about it. I was not too good at it either. I avoided steep slopes and always looked for the easy and safe ones. At that time, there were no ski lifts with chairs, only ropes that one could hold on to, which pulled one up the mountain. I rather walked on my skis (with side steps) up the hill, pulling Eva in her sledge behind me.

Józek seldom came with us to Zakopane. He avoided every sport, as he avoided the sun. However, Eva always chatted up people, men or women, and introduced them to me. Thanks to her, we quickly got company and never felt lonely. We met interesting people like actors, doctors and artists or just ordinary young people, who like us had come with their families to enjoy the sport and sun. Sometimes we stayed four weeks there. I couldn't get enough of it. If I could have, I would have packed this enchanting spot into my luggage and taken it home.

We hired large horse-driven snow carriages, driven by natives called gorals, dressed in long leather pants, fur vests and overcoats. They wrapped us up in heavy, fur-lined blankets and took us for long rides in the woods. The horses had bells around their necks, which sounded like music in the middle of this snowy, fairy-tale-like bushland. The attractions of this trip were the "lake eyes", *Morskie Oko*, crystal-clear blue water lakes in the middle of the deepest snow. What a sight!

I became proud of this country. I loved it for a while even more than Austria. It was my home for next sixteen years. Unfortunately, it was spoiled by the Communists and their Russian influence. As the Polish history shows back to the year 1000 and earlier, this country always had to fight for its independence. They lost and gained lands, but they built a great culture, improving with every century.

The Polish population consisted mainly of Catholics and a small Protestant community. There had been far more Jews before the war, who were all but destroyed. The lucky survivors managed to immigrate to other countries mainly North America.

Józek and I somehow survived there without adopting any religion. We were never seen at church, but no questions were asked. Not even Elspeth asked about it. She, as a German, was a Protestant but never practiced her religion by attending church or other religious services. We kept all holidays like Christmas, Easter and Whitsunday (here in Australia completely unknown). Not even Elspeth, who had no idea we were Jewish, ever suspected anything. Under the Communist regime, churches were not accepted. Unable to ban them completely, religion was taught at schools. Children went to Sunday school out of their own free will. These laws made it easier for us to remain unnoticed.

When Eva was around four years old, I learned from an old friend that Kuba had remarried and immigrated to Palestine. We never got officially divorced, as all the documents were destroyed. I didn't even try to get an annulment. I was not in the slightest keen on another marriage, and neither was Józek. He was so sure of me, my love for him. He was never able to read me, to look into my heart. What you don't know doesn't hurt. I felt my feelings to be private and kept them to myself. Józek made his own laws; for him a marriage license was just a piece of paper.

Yet I had to consider my daughter. She had grown up fast, and in another couple of years would be ready for school. I could not allow her to grow up as an illegitimate child. For her sake, we got married – quietly, as nobody had known otherwise. I had lived under Józek's name Werner ever since I came back with him from Berlin. We treated the marriage ceremony as pure formality. Again, my second marriage took place without having proper wedding arrangements. I could live without that!

My life was never monotonous; this fact was probably written into my fate or put into my cradle.

Another big surprise was waiting: I was pregnant again. What a shock! I had never, ever considered having another child.

24

THE GIFT OF A SON

Always in the back of my mind, I had the fear of losing another baby. We had nearly lost Eva as well. The past was written so clearly in my mind. On the other hand, I had learned to cope with all blows in my life. I had an optimistic nature, and once things happened, I accepted them. After Eva had recovered from her illness, we had moved into the city of Poznań with normal communication facilities.

In Poland, you could buy anything for money but housing. People lived cramped in flats; some larger ones were divided to accommodate two or three families. All blocks of flats were nationalized and hard to obtain. One good thing, though, was that most Polish citizens from the caretaker to the highest officer were corrupt. That was the only way to survive in a Communist country. You could bribe them, and that was exactly what Józek did to obtain a flat.

We considered ourselves very lucky. We got a large apartment, sharing it with three other families. Elspeth and I turned it into a cosy, comfortable living area. I was looking forwards to my new baby, although I was nervous and cranky. Józek and I argued constantly. A couple of weeks before the baby was due, he took off on a holiday with a friend from his hometown, a sleazy, primitive, Jewish man, whom I never wanted to receive in our home. I always had a good intuition when it came to people. A character like him, I knew, was no good company for Józek.

He was using Józek for his own purposes but always delivered what Józek asked. You don't have to guess the obvious; it was the best time for him to have another affair.

Against my will, he took off to a fashionable winter resort. My baby was due around New Year, and Józek left two weeks before Christmas. He must have felt very guilty, as he left me an unusually large amount of money to pay off his bad conscience. Wait, you bastard, I thought, I will pay you back, just wait until after I get back into shape. Promises are made for keeps; they are not supposed to be flexible. I assure you, I kept this promise – did I ever!

Babcia, as we called Eva's grandmother, was as furious at her son as I was. She suggested that Eva and I stay with her and I give birth in Wrocław, where she lived. "You will be well taken care of", she assured me. I knew she meant it, but I did not want to leave; I preferred my own home, my own doctor and my devoted Elspeth. Babcia took Eva with her and kept her out of the unpleasant atmosphere.

Józek rang regularly, and Elspeth always answered the phone, telling him I had left. It spoilt his planned two weeks holiday; he thought I had left him for good. His mother confirmed that I had left, but Eva was staying with her. We all ganged up against him.

He interrupted his holiday and turned up after a week at his mother's. She was a very small lady, even smaller than I am, but she had the energy and strength of two normal-sized women together. When she stood up to her son, she left him speechless, and his arrogance and power went down to zero. She gave him a lecture as never before – Eva told me later all about it. Józek left, feeling down in the dumps, and took Eva home with him; she wanted to be with her mother. He could not believe his eyes when he found me at home, pretending nothing ever had happened.

I had more important things on my mind at that time. With the birth of my baby so imminent, I could not afford any wars with its father.

I planned and prepared the birth at home. My doctor agreed to do it, though home deliveries are unusual in Poland. On 8 January 1955 at 1 a.m., I gave birth (on the dining table) to a big, 4.5 kg healthy boy. His father was sent away with Eva when labour started. I could not imagine having Józek around.

Besides my wonderful doctor and the midwife, my biggest support and help was of course Elspeth. She was the first to hold the baby in her arms after she cleaned him up, and wrapped him in a blanket and looked after him until the doctor finished looking after me. From the first moment on, Pauli became her biggest love and first priority. In my fantasy, I imagined I had gotten my lost baby Peter back. The closest name to it was Paul. When I named the children, I always had in mind that their names would be translated easily into other foreign languages.

Pauli certainly made up for all my losses. He became my greatest love and replaced the love I could never give to his father. I have never stopped loving him; he will always take a big place in my heart. He was a wonderful child, just the contrary to his sister – easy-going, obedient, always keeping quiet in the background.

As for Eva, the older she got, the more difficult she became. She had no jealousy of her baby brother; she adored him as everyone else did. But she stirred up trouble, telling made-up stories, malicious and rude tales in particular about Elspeth. Her father smacked her; I tried to prevent it, as I never believed in physical punishment. She became an unpleasant child, hard to control.

At school, though, she behaved perfectly. She adored her teacher and tried to imitate her in every way. She walked with long steps, spoke in the same loud, domineering way like her and bossed everybody around as teachers do to control their class. Pani Rosińska became her shining example. She was neither pretty nor feminine, but she had a terrific way with children. Eva became the teacher's "pet", and their love was mutual.

Józek took over his daughter's school life and manipulated Pani Rosińska the same way he tried with everybody else. They became close friends. How far this friendship went I could never find out. To be honest, I did not try; neither did I care. At least it was for our daughter's benefit. She always had the best marks and never any complaints at school. I had no desire to investigate my husband's secret love life. With his trip so close to my delivery, I lost all interest in him, most of all my respect.

There was a far more important "Male" in my life: my little son! We all spoiled him, Elspeth in particular, as did his sister and his father. He became the pride in all our lives and warmed everybody's heart when we only looked at him. Pauli took us all for granted. He got our attention, which he wanted and deserved. His biggest love in life, though, was *food*.

Elspeth thought she couldn't reach his heart other than through his stomach, so she stuffed him like a turkey. She smuggled in constantly sweets and cakes, sausages and other fatty foods, all behind my back to please him. Thanks to her, Pauli became addicted to food and obsessive already at an early age. No matter how I tried to convince Elspeth otherwise, she kept on feeding him.

She achieved what she wanted. He became very attached to her, his second mother in every way. There was no competition between us two women. By the way, father and son shared the same eating habits; our good-hearted Elspeth could please them both.

After Pauli was born, I tried desperately to get a flat of our own. To clear Józek's conscience after he went on this trip at the end of my pregnancy, he bought me a second-hand car, a Mercedes 170V.

I somehow received a driver's licence, but I never made a good driver. A taxi driver one day approached us with an offer to buy my car. He invited us to his home to discuss the deal. When I saw his nice flat, an idea popped into my head, I suggested: we could swap flats, and he could take the car as an appreciation for the favour. To our surprise, he agreed. So finally, we could move into our own place from Chełmońskiego to Ulicy Sniadeckich. Many years later, this place would be again swapped for our passports to freedom.

25
LEAVING THE IRON CURTAIN

I hadn't seen my sister Susi for twelve years, and we missed each other. In 1957, it became a bit easier to get out of the country to arrange a family reunion in Vienna. There was one condition; you had to leave close family members behind as a security for your return. I didn't even consider taking Józek with me, but I wanted to show off my children. The authorities refused; I got only a passport for myself. Józek was delighted about this as well, as he feared I could take off with both children. Perhaps I would have. I admit the thought crossed my mind.

I arrived in Vienna a couple of weeks earlier than Susi and had plenty of time to adjust to this new Western world. Freedom, luxury and independence awaited me. Here I was back in Vienna after seventeen years – my native town, where I lived the best part of my life. The past seemed like yesterday, above all the memory of my parents. Although Vienna appeared different, the city itself did not mean much to me. I saw the familiar places I had grown up in, my schools and the home we lived in. Walking the streets where I had lived for almost sixteen years was highly emotional.

I had to relive it alone. Billroth Strasse, number four. The old house hadn't changed. I looked up the balcony on the third floor without the pretty flowerpots my mother used to keep there. She wasn't standing there, waving and laughing, as she used to, when we came back from school. I went inside and saw the same staircase and the same doors with different names on them. The old ones were all gone.

Only the memories were still there. I remembered Papa carrying me all the way up to the third floor, after dancing all night at a ball, when Mutti brought me home by taxi and I was too tired to climb the stairs. I remembered the peaceful and caring atmosphere we were so lucky to grow up in.

Everybody else in life is replaceable: friends, husbands, wives, brothers, sisters, even children. You win some, you lose some. Parents, though, you can never replace. There is only one mother and one father in your life. I knew I had been lucky; I had the best. Knowing that, the memory of their loss becomes more painful. I had to come to terms with that painful past, and I was glad I could experience and overcome it on my own.

I stayed with Auntie Lotte, my father's sister, who thanks to him survived the war in England after her husband was killed in Dachau. She got the factory back, which flourished under the management of an old, loyal employee who had worked for the company before the war. She was a wealthy lady, but after her war experiences, she lived far too modestly considering her circumstances. She had a comfortable three-room apartment in a nice house, and she was happy to share it with Susi and me during our visit.

The reunion with my sister, when we picked her up with Aunt Lotte from the airport, was incredible. We hugged each other so long, crying nonstop, that Susi nearly missed picking up her luggage. We were lost for words, just tears and sobs, all the way home. Susi had changed surprisingly from the chubby, unattractive "Hasha" I had left in Berlin to a slim, good-looking, elegant lady.

I was so proud of my sister. Our "honeymoon" lasted only two weeks. We strolled around Vienna, revisited old places and discovered new ones we hadn't known as children. We had a lot of fun, walking around, holding hands, laughing at typical Austrian people and even joining in their familiar Viennese dialect, which we had nearly forgotten.

We went to shows, movies and a breathtaking performance of Verdi's *Aida* at the Vienna Opera. It was in the months of May, the well-known Viennese springtime, which inspired all the famous composers to write their beautiful music. It put you in a special, optimistic, happy and carefree mood.

Susi became the opposite of myself under her husband's influence: a religious, devout Jew. She was not Orthodox but kept many strict Jewish traditions. She ate kosher and watched for her four hourly breaks between mixing dairy and meat products. She didn't drive on Saturdays or do sewing or housework.

I had known about her practices from her letters, so I was prepared. However, living with her together, watching her unusual lifestyle, the big change in her, she became somehow a stranger to me. We had grown apart in two different worlds. During the first two weeks, I didn't realize that in the trance of finding each other again. I went along with her habits and ate our meals in a primitive and ugly kosher restaurant. It didn't matter to me. Susi tried to convert me, criticizing my non-Jewish life, arguing about my "dropping religion", telling me what a bad person I was. "God will punish you for it, you will see!"

Finally I had enough. Our discussions turned into unpleasant arguments, and we fought all the time. Susi could not have children. She had never really wanted them and put it off for years, and it was too late. For her husband's sake, she tried, but nothing worked. Of course, my children were constantly on my mind. I kept talking about them, telling her how much I enjoyed being a mother. It took me a while to realize how jealous she was! Auntie Lotte opened my eyes and told me to shut my mouth and stop mentioning my children.

It happened that at the same time, Lotte's daughter, my cousin Hedi had her first baby. Hedi and I had been close as children and still got on very well. She was married to a psychiatrist, who had finished his studies when they got married and had been fully supported by Hedi, being a poor student. A couple of days after Susi arrived, Hedi gave birth to her son in the same hospital in which I had been born. I was as excited as her mother and kept visiting her and fussed around the baby. Susi had no interest in it whatsoever. It put her in a bad mood, until I discovered what irritated her.

I slowed down on my visits to Hedi and spent most of the day with Susi. On one of those gorgeous, sunny spring days, we went for a walk into the Volksgarten, one of Vienna's most beautiful parks with artistically arranged flower displays, shrubs and lilac trees. The wonderful aroma there was sweet and strong; it touched not only your nose but also your heart and spirit. We were both in a terrific mood, sitting on the terrace of the Volksgarten restaurant having lunch. I was indulging in my favourite torte with cream when I opened up to my sister.

I told her about Józek and his never-ending affairs, but she did not want to believe me.

I felt close to her for a few moments and began to confide in her about my boyfriend Zdzislaw, my husband had introduced him to me on one of our holiday trips to Krynica. Józek played bridge with him; Zdzislaw wasn't a passionate player but joined in occasionally.

"Would you keep my wife company", Józek asked him, "so I can continue my card games?" Zdzislaw obliged with the greatest pleasure, he later explained to me. He lived in the same private hotel as we did. He took me out for a dinner dance, whilst Eva accompanied her father. Pauli, still a toddler, stayed with Elspeth, who always came with us on our holidays. Zdzislaw was a handsome man, full of life, well-educated, fluent in English. He was an executive manager in a big import–export company. He was married, apparently not very happily (the usual explanation of married men trying to get a woman on their side).

I was interested in him, being bored and looking for company. I didn't care where he came from or about his private life. I was looking for fun and a change, and of course, I hadn't forgotten the promise I made to myself to get back at Józek. This was just the right opportunity.

Józek was fully absorbed in his card games and didn't take any notice what was going on; he did not have the slightest suspicion. The ever-so-clever and jealous husband had no idea how he arranged and made it so easy for the two of us. He could get on with his beloved hobby to play card games all hours. Only Elspeth knew about it. I had not only her approval but all her support. Following all my instructions, she covered up for me, taking good care of the children. We had three exciting and romantic weeks together. I enjoyed every minute of it – one of our best holidays.

Eva was always terrified of mice. We both slept together in one room with her father, and Elspeth in another one at the end of the hallway with Pauli. One night, Józek as usual was playing cards, when I went early to bed with Eva, reading her stories. Suddenly she spotted a mouse running up and down the floor. She screamed and got hysterical, and while I reached for a clothes hanger, she jumped up and down on the bed in my nighty not knowing what to do. Probably I joined into her outrageous screams as well when all hell broke loose. We overheard a knock on the door, and suddenly I saw Zdzislaw standing at the door, watching us and laughing his head off.

In all the years to come, during our happy and close relationship, he kept reminding how he became motivated not to let me go. Everything happening in one's life has got a reason. Zdzislaw actually without knowing helped to keep me going in this unfortunate marriage.

I lived a double life without hurting my children, keeping the family together as long as I could. Zdzislaw gave me confidence and self-assurance, and most of all, he convinced me that not all men were as worthless as I had started to believe. He was just the contrary of Józek, a real gentleman. No feeling of guilt, no regrets, as my priority was still the children. I had no intention of breaking up my marriage because of Zdzislaw. After two years of trying to convince me otherwise, he accepted that we would never be together as a couple.

I explained all that to Susi, but she was shocked and outraged.

Later on, how I wished I had not done it! I told her about my how I had fallen in love and what Zdzislaw meant to me and my life. First she asked for all the details about him – how did we meet, how long had this been going on and what was his background.

"Is he Jewish"? she asked, which maybe would have been acceptable to her.

"No, he isn't Jewish; he is a Catholic who doesn't care about religion". She became abusive and made me feel so low and miserable that I couldn't take it for much longer. From the moment I told her about my new life, her lifelong grudge against me returned.

She had never forgiven me for getting married before her. Then again, whilst she was desperate for a steady relationship in New York, I remarried, long before she even met David. True, she waited longer, made the better choice and was luckier to find a husband like David. Yet without children, her marriage wasn't complete. My confession knocked her out not only for moral reasons, because when it came to men, I was always ahead of her. Of course, she wasn't in the slightest interested in another man, as she was lucky to find David, who was one in a million. She couldn't understand my feelings, as she never even tried when we were children or teenagers.

She showed such contempt and dislike that I couldn't stand the sight of her. What a shame that never in my life could I reach an understanding with my sister. Whenever I had the urge to feel close to her, she knocked me back. I was sure that I would never confide in her again.

26

BACK HOME IN POZNAŃ

I left Vienna far earlier than I had intended with a bitter taste in my mouth. Zdzislaw again cheered me up and made up for it.

Our affair lasted for four years and gave me more strength and an entirely new aspect of life. I still cherish these memories – no regrets whatsoever. So many experiences I would have changed if I could, but this happy episode with Zdzislaw, I wouldn't have had any other way.

I kept a cool relationship with Józek peaceful and friendly for the sake of my children as well as for my own good. I discussed a divorce with a lawyer, my friend's brother-in-law, Danusia. He explained to me that without any proof of physical or mental abuse, I wouldn't have a chance. I discussed the possibility of leaving Józek with this lawyer. He made it clear that I wouldn't be able to keep the children; he had the money and the power.

Józek's first reaction after learning about my intentions was to try to sack Elspeth, to tie me completely to the house and the children. I made it clear that if she were forced to leave, I would join her, no matter what the consequences. He threatened and raged, but finally realized that he couldn't win and dropped the matter. So did I. Divorce was out of the question.

I lived a comfortable life instead, envied by our friends who thought we had a wonderful, harmonious marriage. Even the children believed it. Eva had a close friend at school, Halina. I became friendly with her mother Maria Hetmanowa, who was married to an officer who ruled the house and the children in a military fashion. She wasn't happy in her marriage either. Comparing her life to mine, she always used to say "five minutes before dying, I would love to have a life like yours". Maria was right: you have to make the most of every situation and be optimistic, and it can work. Who cares about unfaithfulness? Józek was my best example.

He could live with it, and so could I. With one big difference – I was discreet so that nobody had any suspicions. My dear husband, though, not only tried to humiliate me, but he wanted to show off his power and cover up all his other weaknesses. No matter what he did and how he acted to put me down, I ended up on top.

I learned a lot in those years about life and about my own ego. Most of all, I learned not to be dominated by a husband or anybody else. On the contrary, I became far more demanding, self-conscious and bossy. I must admit that I liked myself much more that way. As I have a forgiving nature (I don't forget either), it didn't take long to make up with my sister. We started to write to each other again. In the end, we only had each other. She was so full of love and praise about her husband David that I couldn't wait to meet him. She mentioned him in every letter. I should come to visit them, she told me, until I finally, optimistic as I have been (not anymore though), I agreed.

PART 4
TRIP TO
NEW YORK

27

THE "BATORY" VOYAGE

I decided to go with both children to New York. Again, the Polish authorities granted me the departure only with *one* child. Husband and son had to stay back as a "bond". I never considered that Józek should accompany us to America, but I desperately wanted to have my boy with me. It was a big disappointment but, as it turned out later, better for all concerned.

In June 1959, Eva and I left with an old, almost historical ship "Batory", on a wonderful cruise to Montreal via Southampton, Copenhagen and Québec. It was a cruise I will never forget.

Poor Eva was seasick most of the time, although we were lucky and never experienced any really rough waters. The luxury they offered on the "Batory" was far away from any Communist regime. The food was superb, always beautifully presented. I had never seen anything like that before. Most of the time we stayed on the deck, as fresh air was the only cure for Eva's seasickness, so our appetite was tremendous. However, Eva brought up everything, and the crew doctor advised her to cut down on all the tempting sweets and stick to fruit and vegetables. I played table tennis with the crew as there were mostly older passengers who preferred the sun chairs. We swam in the pool – another big attraction that I enjoyed.

At night they had never-ending entertainment and dinner dances, which I hardly attended, as Eva was too exhausted from her sickness. We stopped at Copenhagen for a day and took a sightseeing tour around this beautiful city, so different from all the others I had seen. Eva was too young to understand its beauty, but she enjoyed walking on the ground away from the ship.

28
OLD PORT OF QUÉBEC

Q uébec was another life experience that I will never forget. What an old port, with docks, old residential areas, and architecture so different to the other European cities.

We were told by the ship's officers that women should not walk on their own without male company. Eva and I were not interested in males, so despite all warnings we explored places on our own. It didn't take long for me to find out what the crew had meant.

Men molested and harassed women, in particular tourists, whenever they caught sight of them. The native language in Québec is French. Once again, I had reason to be grateful for my education so I could express my dislike for their intrusion *in French*.

I heard my governess Madame drilling the sentence into my ears: "I don't talk to strangers" (Je ne faux pas parler avec etranger). Some of the men were more understanding than the others. It all depended how full of their Calvados or whatever they drank they were. The men strolling around after lunch were certainly drunk and looking out for women to share their siesta with.

Eva was a great help. She swore at them in Polish and German, something she was always good at. We ran as fast as we could knowing that these drunken swine were too lazy to follow us. When you are frightened, you don't think. That was exactly what we forgot about, being busy with "self-defence".

We got further and further away from our ship in a strange place with strange people. I asked women, avoiding all men, for the directions to the ship. Most of those women were prostitutes. All they knew was where to take the men "to work". Finally we were lucky to get the attention of a more intelligent, understanding older whore. She even spoke fluent English. Batory? Oh yes, I know some of the sailors (did she ever!).

She took us across the city in the direction of the harbour. Time was running out. The ship had only a few hours break and was ready to continue the cruise. We ran, and our guide ran with us. Suddenly I spotted a familiar face in Polish marine uniform. It was our entertainment officer, my daily table tennis partner. He was on his way out to look for us. I had to restrain myself not to hug and kiss him. He took Eva's hand and my arm instead, walking us back like two naughty children. Our helpful whore followed us to see if she could "catch up" with some of the sailors.

Would you believe that even a whore could act as a guardian angel? This was our adventure in Quebec. From that time on I listened to all the advice and rules of the cruise.

29

New York, New York

We arrived in Montreal after eleven days, an eternity for my exhausted daughter.

Susi waited with David in a big crowd at the landing stage for visitors. I spotted David's bald head immediately, sticking out above everybody. He was so tall and noticeable. I only knew him from photos, but I recognized him at once. Next to him, my small, slim sister was like a little doll. We had to wait hours for disembarkation, customs clearance and all formalities. They disembarked in alphabetical order, and with our name Werner, we would have waited forever, if not for my good relationship with my table tennis partners. I turned to one of them asking to release us earlier, considering my daughter, who looked as if she would faint any moment. So we got out first.

In the meantime, Susi and I started a long conversation in sign language, which we had known ever since we were children. We had to fly to New York, she explained. There was no other way, as they had come by plane, not by car as previously planned, to pick us up.

Eva and I were both terrified of flying. We made it somehow. Eva was sick on the plane again but was well looked after by David, who knew exactly what to do with her, like an experienced father would. I was sitting stiff and straight, avoiding looking out the window, squeezing Susi's hand. What an experience coming from Poland!

A much greater excitement was to see New York. Before I started the trip, I had wondered how I would take in the view of all those famous skyscrapers. I have to admit I imagined some scary giants falling on my head. Reality was so much different. Here I walked Wall Street, lined with 40- to 80-story buildings, and it seemed to be very natural. It was grey, not a beautiful sight but not at all frightening. It amazed me how easily we could find places; all the streets and avenues were numbered. Next to Tokyo, it was the biggest city on Earth, but I never got lost there, despite my bad orientation.

I felt like the small, poor county girl coming for the first time to a city, despite growing up in Vienna. Vienna is a village in comparison.

Going back to my home country after almost 20 years, everything had seemed to me so small and boring. So imagine my impression coming from a Communist country like Poland. Warsaw, the capital, was still partly in ruins, building sites everywhere, no department stores, no boutiques, no luxuries. I didn't miss all that at home, but this big contrast in 1959 just overwhelmed me.

The population seemed strange as I hadn't seen many black people before. On the ship, we had befriended a black couple, whose daughter Renee was Eva's age. The girls became friends immediately, and so did I and Renee's parents, the father a doctor of science and the mother also a well-educated lady.

Our first contact in New York was in the subway. I caused quite an upset, when I told Eva in the subway to give up her seat for a pregnant black woman. People were shouting at us from all sides, lecturing us that you don't give preference to black people. Fortunately, my English was so poor in those days that I decided to keep my mouth shut.

My sister lived in an elegant outer suburb, Yonkers, with beautiful two-story houses, villas and mansions. Only rich people settled here, so I was lucky enough to see how the millionaires lived. It wasn't like Hollywood, not extravagant or outstanding, just elegant and tidy. Susi lived with her husband in one of those beautiful houses. They both had excellent taste and decorated the house luxuriously. Susi kept the house spotless; you could have eaten from her floor.

Never-ending housework was not to my liking, I thought; she would have better things to do with her life. What a difference between the space in that big house just for two and our flat in Poland, which we shared with three families. We were worlds apart! I didn't envy her their wealth or luxurious life, just their freedom and independence.

When you haven't lived under a Communist regime, you have no idea how trapped you can be. You could leave the country here, whenever and wherever you like to, and when you return home, nobody will interrogate you about any travel details.

It happened to me, though, when I had returned from my last trip from Vienna. One week later, I was called to the Polish Secret Service (Police Station) where two officers questioned me – similar to a cross-examination in court – for almost two hours. They wanted to know where I had stayed in Vienna, whom I contacted, the names, addresses and other details.

I told them only the truth. I went to see relatives for the first time after the war. They were very interested if I had had any contact with Polish emigres who lived in Austria or other European countries. They asked me about a certain café in Vienna, which must have been known to the Polish police – if and when I visited it. I had absolutely no idea that this particular café was a centre for meetings. I had to assure them again and again that I had had no intention whatsoever of meeting Polish people.

I couldn't tell if they believed me or not, but their proposition was more of a surprise than the interrogation. They offered me free frequent trips to Vienna, first-class hotels, and a lot of money to observe this certain café and report every detail to them. In a word, they offered me the "honourable position of a spy". They kept saying: "You know both languages, you are a woman and nobody will pay any attention to you". What a compliment!

"No, thank you", I answered politely, "I am just a simple housewife, the mother of two children, and I wouldn't come up to your expectations". These two idiots thought I would jump at their proposal. As I signed a declaration that I had been sworn to secrecy, my hand trembled for the first time in my life. My head shook; the whole atmosphere in that room, so clearly in my memory, reminded me of the Gestapo.

Congratulations!

What a flattering offer. Today I can laugh about it, but forty years ago, I was shattered and went to pieces. With every knock at the door, I thought they would come to get me. They didn't, and I never heard from them again.

Nobody in America whom I met could understand that Susi's sister had to live in a Communist country. She and our friends and relatives asked all kinds of questions about it.

You get used to that kind of life, as long as you don't get out and see the difference – and what an enormous difference it was to live here. It was in New York that I made up my mind to leave Poland. I had been brainwashed from all sides to leave Poland, but my sister!

Papa had had a good friend named Leo Lichtblau, a lawyer in Vienna. He had immigrated to New York, and Susi met him there. We both went to see him in his office. He offered me help with immigration to bring the family to America. He assured me, saying: "Your brother-in-law is wealthy enough to guarantee for you"!

Susi became furious at him and started such a fight that I wished I never had gotten in touch with Leo. He meant well for us, and he acted on behalf of Papa. But Susi made it clear that under no circumstances would she even consider bringing my family over to the US.

I have strongly believed in Józek's ability to support us wherever he went. He had proved it again and again. I would never have allowed us to be a burden on my sister and her husband, and never expected their financial support.

I didn't expect this kind of reaction from a sister either. I finally saw clearly what I had not wanted to see, but subconsciously had known all along. Ever since I had been born, I was in my sister's way. For many years, I had to live in her shadow. No more!

She was jealous of me. I had been a threat to her, and she was scared that I would try to take her husband away. Absurd! Yes, David had been wonderful to me from the moment I met him. I saw in him the brother I always wanted, and I loved and respected him, but never ever did I see the "man" in him.

When we were young, we had the same taste in men. I, as the younger sister, always had a crush on Susi's boyfriends. But David? Not for any money in the world would I have even considered flirting with him.

A few days after our arrival, he took me shopping in one of the best department stores.

"I am going to buy you some nice clothes", he said, "without your sister, as she is too stingy to spend money on good things". We walked from his office on 42nd Street to the stores, holding hands to make sure I won't get lost. We were chatting and laughing, when Susi passed us on the bus and probably in her suspicious fantasy got the wrong impression.

Back home, she made me a terrible scene and told me that ever since I had arrived, she had argued with David as never before. Eva was too much for her; she did not intend to "babysit" whilst I was having a good time exploring New York. Eva was exceptionally good and understanding. She was sitting in front of the TV all day, enjoying all the long-running soaps. She got out Susi's way, adjusted to the new rules and the kosher food, and respected and adored David. She never became a burden to anybody but Susi, who didn't understand children.

What a difficult and strange person my sister had become! As hospitable as David was, Susi was just the opposite. Her negative reaction to Leo's persuasion to bring us to America did not come as a big surprise. Probably she did me a big favour that I never tried to immigrate there. For better or worse, our lives would have turned out completely differently.

I stayed from that day on away from her home as much as I could, visiting friends, sightseeing and taking tours, which David and his friends had organized for us.

In the end, we left one month earlier than planned. I stayed a few days with Eva in Montreal until the departure of the Batory..

PART 5

BOOMERANG RETURN TO VIENNA

30

MEETING THE
SECRET POLICE

From all your experiences, good or bad, you learn something new; there is a reason for everything. What I gained from the American trip was a determination to leave Poland.

This idea, injected by Dr Leo Lichtblau, matured more and more in my mind. There had been many times in my life, I have to admit, when I was not sure whether I had made the right decision or not? Many times I knew that I hadn't.

This time, though, I was absolutely convinced that there would be a better future for all of us in the Western part of Europe, away from the Communists, the further the better. I didn't have much choice. The only country with which I was familiar, knew the language of and had some family in was Austria – at least for the time being. I had to plan it thoroughly before I could talk to anybody about it.

A solution eventually presented itself. My Uncle Gutek, Genia's husband, came to Poland for a visit from Brazil after our return from New York. He was an angel sent from heaven at the right time. He took me to the Department of Immigration in Warsaw with the request to bring "*his daughter*" with her family to Brazil.

Again, everything in life has a reason! My idea to take my maiden name after Gutek and Genia Krajewska was one of the best I had ever had. Suddenly I had parents in Brazil, and according to law, the Polish government had to allow the reunion of the closest family. My plan became reality when Gutek put down his official affidavit.

What my sister refused, he did for us with no questions asked and no conditions made. Poor Gutek passed away not long after that of a sudden heart attack in the middle of a conversation with friends. He was in his early sixties, never sick before. What a tragedy for all of us!

When my plan took shape and wasn't just a fantasy anymore, I started the hardest part: convincing Józek. To my great surprise, he agreed immediately.

I didn't know then how deep he had gotten himself again into hot water with his business.

My next step was to go to Vienna to obtain a permanent permit to stay in Austria; we were Polish citizens, only I was born in Vienna. First, I had to legalise my name, which was pretty easy as I obtained a duplicate of my birth certificate. Already on my first visit to Vienna in 1957, Susi and Auntie Lotte had signed a declaration about my real name.

Whilst in Poland, I had been Joanna Maria Werner (Krajewska). In Austria, I became Johanna Werner (Altmann). I had to fill in form after form, and there were endless trips from one department of immigration to another. We needed a guarantor, whom I found in my cousin Fritz, a rich factory owner, well known to the Austrian authorities.

So far so good, but all these formalities took forever as the Austrian bureaucracy was slow and unreliable. To give it a push, I applied for an interview with the Minister of the Interior, Joseph Afritsch.

I was lucky enough to wrap the minister around my little finger when I told him my life story – how I survived the

Holocaust right under Hitler's nose. I just stuck to the truth, which must have touched him deeply. Our conversation took much longer than expected, but I left his office with the assurance that my application would be considered positively. He kept his word, and after a few weeks, I received the permit to settle permanently with my family in Austria.

It was a tremendous step forwards to a completely different life. You can't just sit and wait for your fate to happen. You have to push and try until you get what you want. I have never been so sure about anything in my life as my desire to get out of Poland.

The next and far more difficult step was how to leave. The Polish authorities would never let us go to Austria; it had to be Brazil.

I had, as I already have mentioned, prepared the visa to Brazil via my "father". We had to produce plane tickets for the four of us to Rio de Janeiro. Again I was lucky. During my stay in Vienna, I had worked part time in a Jewish travel office and became friendly with the boss and his wife. Moritz issued those necessary tickets for us, trusting me completely. It was a very generous act, which we could never have done without. Thank you, Moritz for that; I haven't forgotten it after 35 years.

I was 37 years old, full of energy and determination to get what I wanted for my family.

I filled in the waiting time by attending a cosmetic school, the best available in Vienna. I couldn't get money out of Poland; I was only allowed to take $20 in foreign currency, and I did not want to become a financial burden to my family.

In wise foresight, I took some valuable jewellery with me, which I was able to sell to pay for all the expenses. Susi also sent me some money, which helped to pay my school fees.

As she couldn't stop reminding me: "You have to learn a profession"!

I took my studies seriously and I loved the school, the teacher, the girls and best of all the subjects, which seemed tailor-made for me.

After nearly a year away from home and my children, I had to return to organize our departure. As it turned out, there were far more difficulties to be overcome than I had expected. The Secret Police had to have their last say! Every citizen leaving the country permanently had to be stripped to the bone to make sure they hadn't been involved politically and had no criminal record. Endless interviews, waiting time again, forms to fill out. Our permit from Austria was valid only for one year. Time was running out!

31

THE ESCAPE

During my interview with the Secret Police in Posen, I met a nice officer called "Jurek". It was obvious that he tried to help us. I didn't dare to offer a bribe.

Every time I was in his office, someone else was also present: a secretary to take notes, another officer and others. I concentrated on every question he asked to make sure to give the right answer.

One of those questions, which I could not work out immediately, was: "What do you intend to do with your apartment, when you leave"? "We weren't sure yet", I told him, but I couldn't get it out of my mind until I put two and two together.

I knew that Jurek was the most important police officer working on our case, but I had no idea how to approach him. This time fate or coincidence, call it what you like, came to my rescue. I met Jurek at the park close to our home. Was it deliberate or coincidence – did he follow me? I never found out.

As soon as I recognized him, I approached him on the spur of the moment. I said: "hello", and he answered friendlily. We clicked immediately and started a conversation.

"As you are not on duty", I suggested, "and we live so close nearby, why don't you have lunch with us"? To my surprise, Jurek accepted.

After a few drinks and Elspeth's serving one of her delicious meals, I was confident enough to make him an offer *too good to refuse* . He probably had been waiting for it anyway. I promised him our apartment in return for our travel documents. As I expected, he lived with his wife and child in very poor circumstances. Our apartment was luxurious compared to his.

From the moment he asked the question in his office, I had realised what he was after. Intuition? Common sense? I don't know, but I had gotten the picture.

Jurek agreed immediately, and we discussed all the details. As soon as he had our documents ready, he moved in with us. He turned out to be a wonderful friend who not only helped with all the necessary formalities, but took a big part in the moving and packing of our belongings. He even obtained for us a whole railway carriage for all the furniture and luggage, which under normal circumstances we would never have had access to.

We were only allowed to take certain goods out of the country. We couldn't take jewellery, pictures, electrical goods or TVs. Józek and Jurek packed the carriage full of everything we wanted to take. Thanks to Jurek, there was no control; the carriage was locked and sealed after I managed to hide our jewellery and US dollars in the deep corners of one armchair.

What a gamble!

Those sort of risks you could have only taken in Poland, nowhere else!

As we learned later, the next day some members of the Secret Police came looking for Józek, who had been accused of illegal trading. Jurek lost his job for having helped us. He wrote us later, telling us that he had no regrets for what he did. He wanted to get out of the Secret Police anyway. Luckily he wasn't arrested.

We travelled by train, third class, dressed in an ordinary way, so that nobody would take any notice of us. The children were both holding and eating apples (stuffed with our jewellery) just before the last Polish control. They asked their routine questions – if we had any foreign currency or jewellery – and without further investigation, left us alone.

As we crossed the Austrian border, I became hysterical from joy and so relieved. We had finally made it!

First, I collected the apples, some of which were whole, some were half-eaten. All our fortune and diamond rings were hidden in those big red apples. They kept us going for a long time in Vienna. The jewellery, not the apples!

32

STARTING AGAIN

Another chapter of our lives was closed after 16 years in Poland. I was happy and sad at the same time to leave this country. I left some close friends behind. I loved Poland and its people, but hated the Communists! All my children had been born there, two of them buried. My mother had been born in Poland, and both my parents lost their lives there. Poland had played a big part in my life that I could never wipe out. In all my good and bad years, I kept one policy: once a chapter was closed, that was it!

Never to look back, no regrets!

Today, I know, it was the right decision to leave it all behind and start again in Vienna, although Austria had never been a lucky place for me. There was nothing for me to come back to. I never felt at home in Austria after the war, as I do now in Australia. The only familiar thing was the language. The people were strangers; I could never really trust or get close to them.

My marriage with Józek finally broke up two years after our arrival. It had to happen sooner or later. He continued having affairs with much younger women right in front of our noses. Again, no regrets! The most important thing about the divorce was that my children weren't hurt. I never demanded any money, even child support.

I had custody over them, and I made sure they had access to their father whenever they wanted to. Józek had no limitations on his visiting rights. He always had been a loving and caring father.

Elspeth followed us to Vienna six months later. As she had kept her German citizenship ("I am German and always will be", as she used to say), it was easy for her to get out of Poland.

Eva changed for the better. She concentrated on her new school, although it was hard starting with limited knowledge of the German language in middle school. I never pushed her, trusting her as she had never disappointed me as far as school was concerned.

Elspeth and I were the breadwinners. She was again my biggest support in every way. Thanks to my cosmetic diploma, I finally had a profession. I worked as a cosmetic consultant for a company, representing a popular French cosmetic line. I travelled all over Austria, training personnel of retail stores to sell our products. I loved this job, meeting interesting people, mainly women of all ages. On the weekends, I made sure to be at home with my children.

I had close contact with their schools and teachers. At one of Eva's parent-teacher interviews (Sprechtag), I met a former teacher from my own school. What a coincidence! I recognized her immediately. I had gone to a different, private school then, 25 years ago. To my surprise, she remembered my maiden name, the class I had attended and lot of my mates. Amazingly, she remembered my mother as well. What a small world we live in!

Three peaceful years followed after my divorce. I don't know why I had put up with Józek for 18 years. The children didn't seem to suffer, and I finally became free, was my own boss and had a life without pressure and humiliation.

Wonderful!

Of course there were financial problems. I had the responsibility of bringing up my children and making sure they got the right education. Without Józek, who was putting me down and embarrassing me with all his affairs with young girls, mostly sluts, I finally became secure and strong. I convinced myself that I had accomplished a lot by getting us out of Poland, so everything else in future would only be child's play.

Elspeth of course was a tremendous support, I couldn't have done it without her. She had no brains, but a heart of gold. She enjoyed our life without Józek as much as I did. "No man will ever come into our home again", she reminded me. Her loyalty and devotion towards me and the children was unique. We had our little man, Paul, and we three women spoiled him far too much. He quickly became a real Viennese boy; he spoke fluent German with an Austrian accent and became as popular at school as at home.

I avoided men for a long time as I had no intention of getting involved with anyone ever again. Opportunities were still there. I had a friend at work, a good-looking married lady, who tried to convince me that the most wonderful thing in life was LOVE.

She had her boyfriends and affairs, one after the other, she assured me. Men, love and sex keep a woman beautiful and forever young! I couldn't agree.

Probably in the very last corner in my mind was the thought that I wouldn't be alone forever. No matter how I tried to listen to my inner voice, which told me over and over again: "Stay away from men!", there was the feminine, human side in me, which felt lonely. No matter how strong your common sense seems to be, you are always looking for a challenge, excitement and most of all something to look forwards to.

Even if your life seems to be running smoothly and you think you have it all under control, you make mistakes. I, on my part, made plenty of them. I had a good and close relationship with my cousin Hedi, although we were very different from each other. Hedi, with her psychiatrist husband lived, as she called it, in a modern open marriage. They both had their affairs and talked openly about them to each other. As long as Hedi had a partner, everything was fine. When her relationship ended, however, she frequently became less tolerant towards her husband's affairs, and her marriage fell into turmoil. It certainly couldn't work that way.

Her husband, who was enormously stingy, used her financially as much as possible. Hedi might have been strong and different than most women I have known, but she certainly was not stupid. She ended the marriage at almost the same time as I did mine, still keeping a close friendship with her husband Fred. Her appetite for men never slowed down – quite the contrary! She thought they had to be the highlight of every woman's life. Whenever we got together, she tried to convince me that a woman without a partner did not count!

"Zero, nobody is going to take you seriously, appreciate you".

Maybe she was right? At least she put some hints into my head and injected ideas now and then. Not that I hadn't thought about it already before. I always have been honest with myself; I knew that my common sense came second over my feelings.

Finally it happened: I got caught in something!

33

A BLIND DATE

At first I thought, this will be an adventure. Hedi set me up on a blind date with one of her numerous acquaintances.

"I found the right man for you". She seemed very excited on the phone. "He is too slow with his approach to me", she complained. "We have been out a few times, he visited me and nothing happened!" Poor Hedi, she was used to going to bed every time she first met a man.

She knew me too well – that I missed companionship, not sex! Why not? I thought. Let's try just for fun. With my permission, Hedi gave Richard my phone number. I liked his voice on the phone and the way he talked, natural and well-mannered. We met in a small café on the Währinger Gürtel in between our homes. This café used to always be empty in the afternoon, so it was easy to find each other. Hedi had described him to me very accurately. Richard told me later that he had no difficulties in recognizing me either.

My first reaction was "That couldn't be him" – not Hedi's type at all.

That's probably why she wanted to hand him over to me. He wasn't good-looking and not at all dressed for the occasion. Too late to back out, though, he had approached me already!

The moment he started to talk to me, I forgot his looks. He was charming and witty and very entertaining. He reminded me of the actor Heinz Rühmann, who wasn't a "good looker" either, but captivated his audience in his movies and theatres for more than half a century.

What the heck, I thought, a man does not have to be handsome! We clicked immediately. He took me out and told me honestly his life story. He was still legally married, but had been separated for the last five years. He had recently broken up with a woman with whom he had had a three-year relationship. He had noticed, of course, the big difference in personality between my Hedi and myself, which seemed to surprise and please him. Hedi was not his "kind of woman", he confided in me. He was the proud father of three sons, the oldest his stepson. He talked nicely about his wife, eleven years his senior. He encouraged me to talk about myself and was a good listener. We spent the most interesting and appealing afternoon and long evening together.

Richard was a gentleman through and through. His personality was amazingly different from all the other men I had met. It wasn't love at the first sight on my part, but I enjoyed his company tremendously.

Although he was a busy owner of three shops, he always took time to see me every day when I was not travelling. He even took me by car to my various business destinations all over Austria.

Cars never meant anything to me, but it seemed odd when Richard turned up with an old station car on our first date. He apologised that his second car had needed to be serviced. What a surprise mixed with relief when Richard picked me up from my house the next day. His Alfa Romeo not only caught Paul's watchful eye and made him shout for joy, but suddenly one head after the other appeared in the neighbours' windows. Our street was not used to luxury cars like that.

I also noticed my customer's attention as we turned up in that car, and he received VIP treatment at the hotel receptions.

Nobody could ever call me a snob, but I must admit that my self-confidence got an enormous lift!

What a difference it makes for a woman if she is single or accompanied by a gentleman with an expensive car. Richard's courtship was attentive, loving and caring. It was almost too good to be true. I couldn't help but fall in love with him.

You can fall in love many times, but you really love only once in your life. My real love was the first one; now I can see it so clearly, even if I thought I had put it all behind me.

But Richard was my final destination. He was and still is a gentleman, faithful and loyal. From the day we met, he never looked at another woman, as I have never been interested in another man. He wasn't bossy either; on the contrary, I took the reins from the beginning.

The children accepted him. Paul was so taken by his car that the "uncle" became his good friend. Eva, though, was terribly shaken that her mother "at her age" (I was 42 then) could have fallen in love again. When Józek came to visit, she cried on her father's shoulder that mum was in love like a teenager!

She and her boyfriend Gerd kept following us at night, when we went out together, to find out how far the relationship had gone. When I stayed overnight at Richard's place, we pretended I was away on a business trip, and we parked the car a few streets further away from home. We had to play this game for quite a while, as Elspeth did not approve of this new situation. She couldn't come to terms with her beloved Frau Werner getting involved with a man again!

What seemed to be right then seems to me completely different now. When you are young and make mistakes, it's part of growing up, but when you reach a mature age and keep making the same mistakes, you have to pay for it!

All this awareness, though, came much later. Eva quickly adjusted to the new situation after she had overcome the initial shock. She soon realized that Richard was genuine and did not interfere in her or her brother's life. From the beginning of our relationship, I made it quite clear that I would not tolerate any interference from Richard where my children were concerned. Richard accepted it and never even tried to do so.

Today I wish he would have, perhaps, as they would treat me with more respect and appreciation. They had too much liberty; I always went along with all their wishes. Without a word to the children, their father suddenly left for Israel, where his mother and sisters had lived already for many years.

Top secret!

He left his Pekinese dog *Putzi* with his landlady and a letter explaining that the dog belonged to us. What a generous "good-bye" present! A dog was the last thing we needed as an addition to our family. Typical Józek! No questions asked, just orders. The last order he gave to me.

The children were devastated – what a terrible disappointment! Who would have thought that a good father like Józek would take off and leave the children without taking any responsibility to pay his share for their education? Vienna wasn't a good place for him to make a living. He had been used to his own rules, his own laws. Vienna wasn't Poland, where he used to turn with the wind. Vienna looked for experts, and you had to prove you were one. We were not entitled to the Austrian citizenship and needed working permits. Józek never applied for one; I got mine extended every six months with the help of my boss.

At first I thought his departure was because of me. He had left so suddenly, and he always told me that if he found me with another man, he would kill me. Well, Józek had many faults, but he had no killer instinct. He did stir at the beginning of my relationship with Richard. He called him a playboy and predicted it would never last. But I don't think I was the reason he had left. He needed family support and friends; he could have never made it in Vienna.

But Józek and Israel? Not long before, I would have thought it would be the last country he would have turned to. He must have been really desperate, but I have to admit that for him, it was the only solution.

Good riddance!

It was a blessing for the poor dog, which Józek had fed only chicken heads. We all loved and spoiled our *Putzi* for many years. He reached the age of 18 before he finally had to leave this strange world.

Elspeth and our dog Putzi in Vienna. He lived to be 18 years old under her wonderful care.

34

WEDDING BELLS

On 8 September 1967, the same date we had met two years before, Richard and I got married in a simple ceremony at the registry office. It was my third marriage with no real wedding. We just needed a piece of paper to legalize our relationship for the kids' sake.

I came to the conclusion that I couldn't live in two houses, as I had for the last year.

I had rented out one room of our apartment, which helped to pay the rent and made ends meet. I had no alternative other than to stay in Richard's small flat. In the meantime, Elspeth was running the house confidently and absolutely in control. She looked thunderstruck as we announced our plan to get married. As loyal and attached she always had been to our family, she made no demands for herself. She had only one wish: to have a place of her own. Now was the time to make her dream become true. We thought to win over Elspeth by offering Richard's flat to her after we got married, which he could have sold otherwise.

Her reaction was as unexpected as it was illogical. She burst into tears and misunderstood our good intentions. She thought we were throwing her out and she wouldn't be needed anymore! It took me a long time to convince her that she would be still the same precious member of our family and, at the same time, free to live her own life in the privacy of her own home.

It didn't take her long after moving in to her comfortable, nicely furnished flat to settle in happily with Putzi, whom she insisted on taking with her.

As it turned out a few years later, we couldn't have given her better security for the rest of her life. She still kept the same control over housekeeping and her beloved Pauli. She kept on feeding him all the wrong fattening foods, as she did for years, contributing to his obesity – something we never agreed on and which caused many arguments between us. As we say in German: "Liebe geht durch den Magen". For a long time, she didn't realize what harm she was doing to him despite her good intentions.

As for me, with this marriage I had made another big mistake for which I will never forgive myself. Richard was a good-natured gentleman. That's what made me fall in love with him. I was flattered by all his attention. I thought: "Finally I am going to live a normal and secure life". Most of all I was taken by the way he accepted and supported my children.

Yet all these traits were not enough for an everlasting love and relationship.

We were just not compatible!

I was to blame as much as he was. I didn't know then that to be in love and to love truly is a tremendous difference. I never took a man seriously enough to "look up to him". No matter how hard I tried to adjust to a marriage, it was out of loyalty and trying always to "do the right thing". Just as quickly as I had fallen in love with Richard, I later felt bored and disinterested.

Once again, I had made the wrong choice. Serves me right! I found myself tangled in a web of problems. He had debts and was completely financially insecure. Richard's problems became my problems, and boy, did he have heaps of them!

Richard was honest enough to tell me about his financial situation right from the start, but optimistic as I was back then and all my life before, I thought we were going to manage somehow.

We didn't: there was no future for us in Vienna, not for us and not for my children. Money is not everything, but it helps tremendously. When we found ourselves on the verge of bankruptcy, I found the solution.

35

THE LAND DOWN UNDER

Eva had a workmate who she brought home one day for dinner named Eve.

Eve was a nice, intelligent girl, who lived in Melbourne with her Australian mother. She had come to Vienna on a working holiday and got a job at my friends' travel agency, where Eva worked part time. The owner of the agency, Moritz, always took in people from all over the world.

That evening, Eve M. told us a lot about Australia. Life there was easy, with hardly any bureaucracy, a county with mixed culture and languages. For a small deposit, you could get your own house, or you could rent a flat wherever it suited you.

What a difference between the housing shortage in Austria and over there, I thought. She told us about the beauty of Australia, with beaches and untouched nature. She talked about the friendly people and their sense of compassion, support and consideration for their fellow human being. Social security and a care for the elderly were all in place.

I couldn't hear enough of it. Eve M. had such a terrific talent to bring across her story vividly that I was completely taken by this part of the world. I never had really heard or read about it in detail. All I knew were geographical and historical facts we had learned at school about that faraway continent.

The classrooms in our middle school were named after the five continents. My classroom was called *Australia*. Who would have thought then?

After Eve M. left that night, I could hardly find any sleep. Australia was on my mind from that day on. Slowly I put bits and pieces together in my mind until my idea was born. Finally I could see a small light out of the labyrinth I had gotten myself into again by way of matrimony.

Was it already fate in my life?

When you can't make it in one place, you try to make it somewhere else.

When the ground keeps burning: run! As long as you can swim, you don't drown. We had to start yet again from scratch, but I thought, so what? One more time or less, what difference does it make? Did I ever call a country my "home country"? No! I have never been patriotic either. As far as I was concerned, I would call home a country where I could live happily after.

Now, how to tell Richard? Apart from German, he had no knowledge of any other language. What would his reaction be? There was no harm in trying to persuade him.

Would it be the right place for my children? They would have a far better future in Australia. Eva had gotten married and divorced after only a few months. It would help her a lot to forget about it completely. She had just met a new young man, and she was in love again! We could get them around all right, I thought, if they were serious about each other.

Paul had just turned 16, still very immature, but a good-natured child. He didn't like to study like his sister, and I didn't force him to it, either. He could learn a trade over there or continue school; everything was open to negotiation.

What about our friends? We would make new ones. Well after all these exciting thoughts, chaotic first and becoming more organized and realistic, I waited for the right moment to fill Richard in on my plans.

I had only known him for five years, but I knew him pretty well. He always said "no" first, and in the end, he went along with my ideas most of the time. His initial reaction was of course negative. In his kind and gentle way, he was against it. I gave him time and didn't pressure him to make a decision. I was determined to go for it.

Now looking back, 29 years later, I am convinced it was the best idea I ever had. One day, out of the blue, Richard told me that he had changed his mind; he was ready to emigrate. We went together to the Australian Immigration department and got all the brochures and applications forms. No harm in applying; we could always change our mind, I encouraged Richard.

Everything came so easily in those days. After a couple of months, the three of us (Richard, Paul and I) were advised by the Immigration office to come for an interview.

Eva did not apply, as she couldn't decide to leave without Victor. It was out of the question for him to leave his home country.

The interview was simple. Most of the time, I had to do all the talking as the officer in charge tested our knowledge of the English language. One person had to speak moderately well, and that was me. I was far from perfect, but spoke enough to satisfy their demands.

Six weeks later, after providing all the necessary documents, we received our permit to go to Australia.

PART 6

LAST STOP: AUSTRALIA

36

FIRST AUSSIE GENERATION

When the phone rang at six o'clock in the morning, I immediately knew what was happening.

"Good news already?" I asked when I answered the phone.

"No, not yet, I have just brought Eva to the hospital". Victor's usual calm voice had an immediate positive effect on my tense nerves. Eva had gone into labour. "We will be there shortly", I answered, ready to put the receiver down.

"Just wait a few hours", Victor insisted. "She has still a long time to go, save your nerves for later". I got jumpy and impatient and didn't know what to do with myself. I would go anyway, I decided, and banged on the bathroom door to make Richard hurry. It was the first time I would be a grandmother, and I wanted to be there with my daughter.

The maternity wing of the Private Mercy Hospital looked more like an elegant hotel than a hospital. What a comparison to a hospital in Vienna, not to mention Poland. The peaceful surroundings lifted my spirits immediately, and my nerves settled down.

After a short visit and a quick talk to Eva, a nurse took me to a small waiting room. I sent Richard back home and prepared for a long wait. There I had plenty of time to refresh my memories. I was the only one in the room.

Summing up our lives over the last four years, I came to the conclusion that we all had faced a monumental task by moving to Australia.

Richard, Paul and I had arrived on Cup Day in November 1971 in Melbourne. Since we were travelling with enormous luggage (34 TV boxes, besides numerous suitcases), the organizer of the Immigration Department had to get instructions from the government about the huge transport of our belongings. The friendly and helpful man got his instructions to hire as many taxis as necessary to take us to the migrants' hostel together with our bits and pieces.

Halfway from Tullamarine Airport to Maribyrnong, Richard remembered that he had left his camera at the airport. A friendly taxi driver immediately turned back to the airport, whilst the rest of the procession with our luggage moved on. I offered to pay him for the additional trip, but he stopped at the nearest phone box (no car or mobile phones were available then) to get the government's permission and he did.

What a great country!

Richard found his camera in the same place where he had left it. The first impression is always the best. All those little first experiences in this unknown part of the world made me love Australia from the start.

Love at first sight!

The hostel seemed to be the best accommodation available for us at that time. The only unpleasant experience we had there were with other migrants. All Australians we had to deal with were marvellous. Six weeks later, Richard and I both had jobs, and we moved into a nice, rented flat in Thornbury. We had to start from scratch!

We had to learn to live in a new country with new customs. I did all my shopping in a milk bar until I was told about "super-markets". One of my neighbours, a young female tram conductor, filled me in on everyday needs and provided practical advice. I learned from her a whole new way of living, so different from our life in the past.

From the very start, which was a good one, I put my past behind me, as I always managed to do when starting a new life. When you are determined to make the best of a situation, you can do it!

All three of us joined English classes in a government-run migrant school. Our teacher happened to be a funny Jewish gentleman from Austria. He became fond of Paul, and besides English, he taught him a lot about life as a migrant. His influence on Paul was excellent, and they developed a close "father-son" relationship.

Paul missed his father, his friends and his sister. He found it the hardest to adjust to his new life. He picked up the language in no time, and thanks to Mr Elisher, his pronunciation improved so much that you could hardly notice his Austrian accent. After Richard and I settled into our jobs, the next step was to find the right profession for Paul.

In Georges, the most fashionable and expensive department store in Melbourne, where I worked, I learned more and more about Australian lifestyle and the Australian people. As I always kept my ears open, I was told by a workmate that a lot of Australians of all ages were wearing dentures as dentists charged a fortune for crown work.

Also, people hated drilling, fillings and other unpleasant dental procedures. The easiest way out was extraction of all teeth under local anaesthesia. Not only did you never have to suffer again, but you got yourself one or two sets of new, white and shiny beautiful teeth. That's the way it looked to the average person, who had no idea what you get yourself into when you start wearing dentures.

It clicked in my mind that Paul could become a dental technician. He didn't want to finish high school; he wanted to learn a profession to earn a lot of money. Of course, as Paul was (and is) always against whatever I had to say, he did not agree at the start. He had set his eyes on repairing air conditioners. Thank God, I put my foot down, and Mr Elisher supported me. So finally Paul found an apprenticeship with an older technician, Mr Jack Cooper.

He learned the trade, joined the technical school and took his job and responsibilities seriously. He even enjoyed his new job. What he didn't like, though, were house rules.

I worked twice a week till nine p.m. and Saturday mornings. We had no car in the first eighteen months after our arrival. Everybody had to chip in with the housework, which Paul ignored. He preferred to sleep until noon, before he started his apprenticeship. After he got a regular income, which wasn't much, but enough to contribute a part of it to our household, he quit!

He left home when he was seventeen years old, and there was nothing I could do about it. It was his legal right. As heartbroken as I was then, I know today, it was for him the best thing to do. The spoiled, pampered little boy worked hard at night and weekends as a waiter, until he worked his way up to buy a dental technician business.

In the meantime, Eva got married, still in Vienna, and after a long and hard persuasion, she convinced Victor to join us in Australia.

They came in April 1973, just in time for my 50th birthday. For them, it was already easier, as they had a prepared home with us, a big step ahead to guide them.

Eva had a good knowledge of English, but Victor couldn't speak at all. We had prepared a job with a big German company for him, where Bob, a friend of ours, recommended him.

As Victor had worked at the same company already in Vienna, he got a position straight away. He studied the language intensively, and like Paul, he was a fast learner. However, he kept his very strong accent until today.

The only one who couldn't learn it was Richard. He worked as a TV technician, but neither his bosses nor customers were impressed with him. He was lucky, though, that his workmates, particularly Barry who had an aboriginal background, covered up for him.

Call it fate or luck or just another coincidence, I answered an advertisement in *The Age Newspaper*. They were looking for a temporary replacement for an owner in a TV workshop. Talking to the man on the phone, I immediately recognized his Polish accent. As I continued our conversation in Polish, I told him that Richard was Austrian. Stan was delighted.

We went to see him in Altona to inspect his business. Soon after that Richard took over running it. I went with Richard every day, as I had to do the talking while he did the work. For three months, Richard was his own boss, and he liked that. He had a few German and a lot of Polish customers. There Richard really practiced and learned the trade from experience, but not always to the customers' satisfaction. After Stan came back to take over again, our mind was made up. We started our own TV service.

My thoughts were interrupted when Victor came out of the delivery room to tell me that everything was going slowly, but normally with Eva's delivery. It was a tough job for my girl. Eva had gone through a difficult time during her first pregnancy. She went to see her dying father in Israel, who passed away before her child was born. Later she told me that it was his dying wish for her to start a family.

He said, while gravely ill in hospital, that the most important thing in life was to have children. After that trip, she became pregnant within a month, just to let him know that he was to be a grandfather. It broke her heart later, knowing he never lived to see the happy day.

I got the doctor's permission to see Eva for a few moments. She cried when she saw me. "Mum, why didn't you tell me it would be so hard?'

I wished I could have finished the job for her. Finally it all came to an end, and she gave birth to a beautiful baby girl, Jessica.

"Make sure her grandmother is going to give her a cuddle before the trip to the nursery", I heard the doctor saying. So here she was, my first grandchild, as I wished so much, a grand-daughter. From the first moment that I held this precious baby in my arms, I knew I was going to love her more than anybody in the world. She was my number one!

Having your first child is the most wonderful experience for a mother. Becoming a grandmother, though, is a feeling you just can't put into words. You feel once again so very protective. Once your children have grown up, they slip away from you. They have to live their own, sometimes very different lives. They chose their partners, who are complete strangers to you or your heart is not in it.

Your grandchild is a brand new baby, your flesh and blood, and for me, they became the most important and beloved people in my life. I could never have loved a man with such a passion as I love my grandchildren. Three grandsons were to follow; the first of these was Jessica's brother Oliver, three years later.

During Eva's second pregnancy, with Oliver in 1978, I went back to Europe. During my visit to Israel to see my sister Susi, I met with my first husband, Kuba.

Boy, how he had changed! He looked old, bald and ugly. All he had kept was his charm.

My son Paul got married and had two sons, my two grand-sons Andrew and Robert. My four grandchildren are very different from each other, but to me, they are as special as they were the day they were born.

37

REFLECTIONS

Summing up my life, I can honestly say I have always been lucky! What a miracle that I survived the Holocaust without being in a concentration camp. I survived the loss of my beloved parents and two babies. I had been heartbroken having lost my youth, but I always got out of my misery. I always had the strength to start over again. My stubbornness, my instinct for people and my "nose", which always can smell dishonesty far ahead, helped me to survive.

Men have been always part of my life, but I never took them really seriously. After Kuba, I was never madly in love again. That experience helped me to look right through other men, and when the time came to let them go, I had no regrets. Another encounter ended, and I got out of it a little bit older and quite a bit wiser. No man is worth losing a tear over them. Except my son and all my grandsons, who I don't throw into the same category.

The best thing I achieved in my life was our immigration to Australia, the best country in the world! For the last 29 years, I have never been homesick. I only wish I would have come here earlier. I had so many ups and downs in my life, but I always found a way out. I kept going when I had to go, until I reached my last stop: AUSTRALIA.

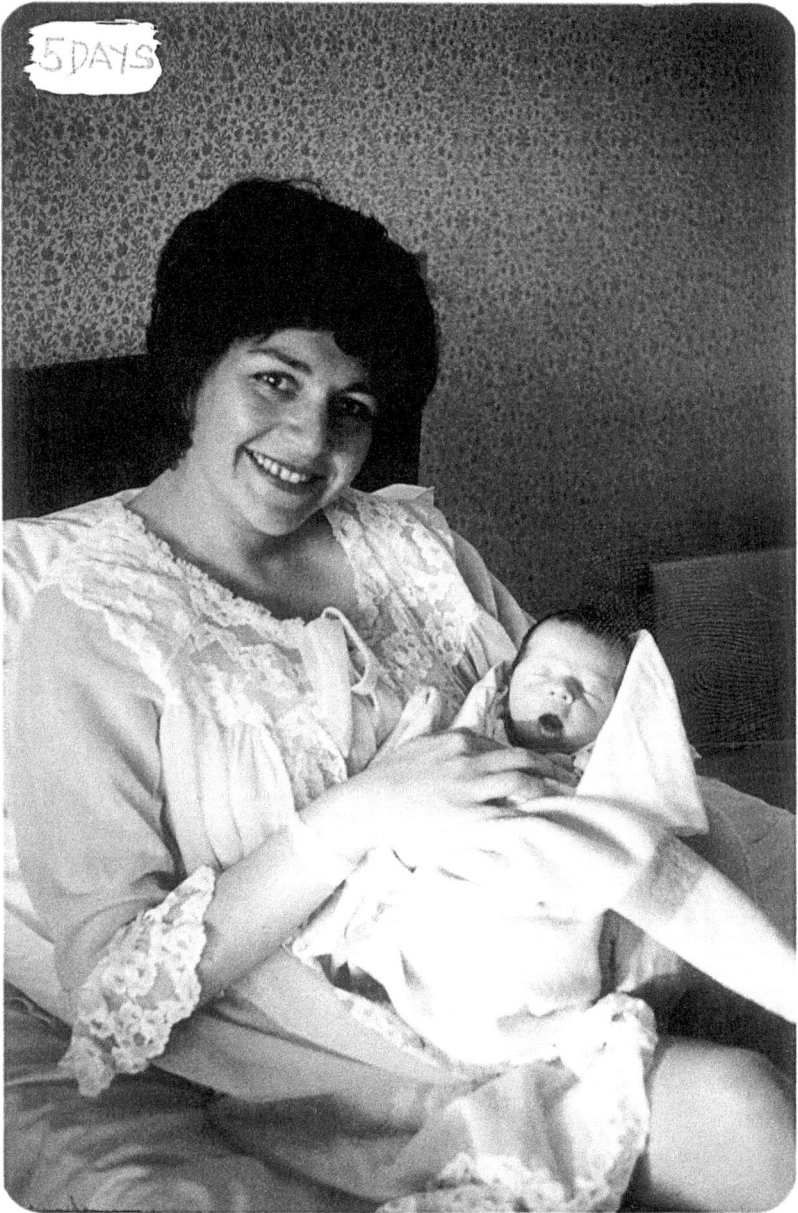

Eva and Jessica, first Australian born member of the family in 1975.

ACKNOWLEDGMENTS

I wish to thank my daughter Eva, who originally typed this manuscript in the late 1990s and lost the diskette. She had to do it all again in 2015.

In 2016, I wished to have this book published, so Eva decided to master the skill of publishing. With her help, New Homeland Publishing was established.

I wish to thank Julie Postance, a book publishing consultant from Inspire Media, for her guidance and support in making my dream a reality.

I wish to thank my grandchildren Oliver and Jessica for their encouragement and for dealing with the photos, creating a lasting memory for the next generations.

I wish to also thank my son Paul, his wife Trish and my grandsons Andrew and Rob who look after me so that I can continue enjoying a peaceful and happy life.

ABOUT THE AUTHOR

Johanna Altmann is now 93 years old and lives in Melbourne, Australia. She wrote this book in her seventies when her manual handwriting skills were still in top order. Her physical health is now fragile, but her mind is as sharp as ever.

This is a true record of her long life, which was full of challenges but also great joys.

www.ingramcontent.com/pod-product-compliance
Lightning Source LLC
Chambersburg PA
CBHW071846090426

42811CB00035B/2349/J